T0051408

Joshua Davis

SPARE PARTS

THE **TRUE STORY** OF FOUR **UNDOCUMENTED TEENAGERS**, ONE **UGLY ROBOT**, AND AN **IMPOSSIBLE DREAM**

Adapted for Young Readers by **Reyna Grande**
Afterword by the Author

FARRAR STRAUS GIROUX

NEW YORK

Adapted for young readers from *Spare Parts: Four Undocumented Teenagers, One Ugly Robot, and the Battle for the American Dream* by Joshua Davis, published by Farrar, Straus and Giroux in 2014.

Farrar Straus Giroux Books for Young Readers
An imprint of Macmillan Publishing Group, LLC
120 Broadway, New York, NY 10271 • mackids.com

Our books may be purchased in bulk for promotional, educational, or business use. Please contact your local bookseller or the Macmillan Corporate and Premium Sales Department at (800) 221-7945 ext. 5442 or by e-mail at MacmillanSpecialMarkets@macmillan.com.

Library of Congress Cataloging-in-Publication Data

Names: Davis, Joshua, 1974– author. | Grande, Reyna, abridger.
Title: Spare parts : four undocumented teenagers, one ugly robot, and the battle for the American dream / Joshua Davis ; adapted for young readers by Reyna Grande.
Other titles: Spare parts (Adaptation)
Description: First edition. | New York : Farrar Straus Giroux, 2023. | Adaptation of: Spare parts / Joshua Davis. New York : Farrar, Straus, and Giroux, 2014. | Audience: Ages 10 to 14 | Audience: Grades 4–6 | Summary: "The young readers' edition of the bestselling adult book of the same name"— Provided by publisher.
Identifiers: LCCN 2022043414 | ISBN 9780374388614 (hardcover)
Subjects: LCSH: Robotics—Competitions—United States—Juvenile literature. | Remote submersibles—Competitions—United States—Juvenile literature. | Mexican American boys—Education—United States—Juvenile literature. | Mexican Americans—Economic conditions—Juvenile literature. | Phoenix (Ariz.)—Social life and customs—Juvenile literature.
Classification: LCC TJ211.26 .D385 2023 | DDC 629.8/9207979173—dc23/eng/20221026
LC record available at https://lccn.loc.gov/2022043414

First edition, 2023
Book design by Samira Iravani
Printed in the United States of America by Lakeside Book Company, Harrisonburg, Virginia

10   9   8   7   6   5   4   3   2   1

For Allan Cameron, Fredi Lajvardi, and America's teachers,
all of whom are on the front lines of the American Dream

FROM LEFT: Lorenzo, Luis, Oscar, and Cristian in Philadelphia in 2005, in front of the Liberty Bell

PART ONE

LORENZO

LORENZO SANTILLÁN WAS A BABY WHEN HIS MOTHER DROPPED HIM ON his head. It was already shaped like a pear. Now he had a big bump growing on his forehead. His mother was worried. There weren't good hospitals in Zitácuaro, their little town in the Mexican state of Michoacán. So she snuck the baby across the US–Mexico border through an underground tunnel to get him better medical care.

A doctor in Phoenix, Arizona, took a look at Lorenzo and said that surgery could fix his skull but might harm his brain. "As far as I can tell," the doctor said, "Lorenzo is doing fine. Why risk it?"

From that moment on, Lorenzo's mother always told him that the bump above his right eyebrow meant he was smart. "Your extra brains are in there!" she said.

Now that they were in the United States, they stayed. The family was barely getting by in Michoacán, but in Phoenix, his father could make five dollars an hour as a gardener. The only problem was that they didn't have permission to stay. Without legal immigration status, they would join the millions of undocumented people living in fear of being arrested or sent back to their countries. But it was worth the risks.

They moved into a two-room apartment in a poor neighborhood near downtown Phoenix. It was very different from Zitácuaro, where Lorenzo's father could search the forest for food—skunks, squirrels, and iguanas that his mother would make into a delicious stew. Now they were starting a new life in the middle of a big city, and they couldn't hunt for dinner. They were stuck eating mostly beans.

His mother got a part-time job as a hotel maid. His father did gardening work under the burning Arizona sun. The family grew. Lorenzo and his older brother, José, had been born in Mexico, but soon, new children came into the family—Pablo Jr., Yoliet, and Fernando—born in the United States and automatically American citizens. While Lorenzo and the rest of his family didn't have papers, his two younger brothers and sister had US birth certificates and social security numbers, which meant they would have opportunities—like legally living and working in the United States—that Lorenzo could only dream of.

His mother loved her new life, and Mexico soon became a faded memory for her. But his father never forgot the peace and quiet of the Mexican forest. Now he found himself in a new country with five children to feed. At night and on weekends, he would come home with a twelve-pack of beer. Lorenzo would watch him drink his way through it. His father got emotional when he was drunk. Sometimes he told Lorenzo, "I love you, mijo." Other times he snapped. One day, he asked Lorenzo to clean up the living room. Lorenzo refused—he hadn't made the mess—so his father grabbed an extension cord and went after him.

That wasn't the first or last time Lorenzo received a beating from his father.

AS LORENZO GOT OLDER, HIS CHEEKS FILLED OUT, BUT THE TOP OF his head stayed small. Kids made fun of his pear-shaped head, and when he got to middle school, they also laughed at his unibrow. Many days, he came home crying.

The other boys at school all seemed to have short hair and nice fades, but not Lorenzo. His family couldn't afford a barber, so his mother cut his hair at home. One day, he decided he needed a new look.

He asked his mom to trim just his bangs. Except for the top, he let the rest of his hair grow out, and soon it reached his shoulders.

"It looks really nice," his mom said.

His classmates didn't think so. Sometimes they called him an egghead, other times El Buki, after a long-haired Mexican pop singer. When they called him a girl, Lorenzo fired back that he was more of a man because he could take all the insults.

"I don't want to be like everyone else!" he yelled, trying to pretend it didn't hurt. He was different, and there was nothing he could do about it.

CRISTIAN

CRISTIAN ARCEGA TRIED NOT TO CARE WHAT ANYONE THOUGHT OF him. But it was hard. He was short, skinny, and not good at the things that got you noticed among kids his age. He couldn't tell jokes. He couldn't play soccer without tripping over his own feet.

Being short meant it was easy for others to push him around. He decided it was safer to stay inside, away from bullies, and play with things that couldn't push back.

Except sometimes they did. When he was four years old, Cristian took apart the family radio and snapped a few internal wires with a fork. What would happen if he broke the connections and then plugged it back in? When he flipped the power switch, the radio popped with a bright electric flash, and the lights went out. The house was thrown into darkness.

His mother rushed in and grabbed him. "¿Pero qué estás haciendo?"

As she asked him what he was doing, he could only think one thing: *Wow, that was fun!*

Soon, other household appliances ended up in pieces. He wanted to take things apart and see how they worked.

When he turned five, he declared, "I want to build robots!"

Nobody in the family was surprised about this—or knew how to help him. His school, in a poor neighborhood in Mexicali, Mexico, was built of wooden shipping pallets. His parents hadn't finished elementary school and had little interest in computers and other machines.

One day, Cristian's father left his job at a vegetable-packing factory and crossed the border to find work in Arizona. The money was better, but he missed his family. Cristian missed his dad, too. While he was gone, he busied himself by building things out of lumber scraps and rusted nails—from helicopters that wouldn't fly to race cars that barely rolled. His father was pretty sure that in Mexicali, Cristian wasn't going to get to learn to build robots. In the United States, he might have a chance.

At five years old, Cristian was driven across the border. He slept through most of the mysterious journey. When he woke up, he was in Yuma, Arizona. His family explained nothing about the illegal crossing. They just kept driving another two hours east until they reached the small town of Stanfield, Arizona, fifty miles south of Phoenix.

With only six hundred people, Stanfield might have seemed like a ghost town. Tumbleweeds blew through vacant lots. There were few homes, and many of them were boarded up. Everything was brown except for the little patches of green farmland in the middle of the wide, empty Sonoran Desert.

Cristian's father and another family had rented an old house with torn-up shutters and holes in the walls. The roof was full of holes, too, but luckily it didn't rain much. There wasn't enough space for both families, and so they all crammed together in three dusty rooms.

Cristian started school that December at Stanfield Elementary. A sign out in front of the brick buildings had a picture of a roadrunner, the school's mascot. It seemed like a welcoming place, but Cristian couldn't speak any English. On his first day, he was seated at a desk among the other students. His teacher chattered away, but Cristian didn't understand a word she said. When the teacher passed out a worksheet, he couldn't make sense of the English instructions. He looked over at a girl sitting beside him, but she said something mean and covered up her work.

At the end of the day, he was supposed to take the school bus home. But when he walked out to find it, he saw a long row of yellow buses. Which one had his mother told him to take? He saw a girl he recognized—he had seen her playing at a neighbor's house—so he followed her onto a bus.

The bus drove and drove. Nothing looked familiar. When the girl got off, Cristian didn't see his house anywhere, so he didn't move. Finally, he fell asleep.

"Kid, wake up," a voice said. Cristian opened his eyes and saw the driver leaning over him. He was the only student left on the bus. It was dark out. He had been on the bus for a long time.

"Where do you live?" the driver asked.

Cristian showed him a slip of paper. His mother had written out the address. The man laughed and said something. Cristian got the gist: "You're on the wrong bus, kid."

Luckily, the man went out of his way to drive him home.

OSCAR

OSCAR VAZQUEZ WOKE UP ONE WINTER MORNING TO THE SMELL OF burning pine and oak. He got out of bed to see a huge fire in the backyard. A big pot of water was boiling up clouds of steam into the early-morning air. He knew this meant his father was going to butcher one of the pigs. In addition to four cows, two horses, a colt, and a mule, the family had three pigs. The sacrifice of one of them meant something big was happening—like a party! Oscar was thrilled.

He was nine years old and lived in Temósachic, Chihuahua, in northern Mexico. It was a town of about a thousand people and two cars. The roads were dirt and the people poor, but they knew how to throw a party. He was sure there would be lots of kids, games, and carnitas tacos, Oscar's favorite.

He went outside just as his father was leading the pig from its pen. He handed the tether to Oscar. "Jala, mijo," his father told him.

Oscar pulled as hard as he could. He'd seen animals killed before, but he'd never been part of it. "Am I going to help butcher it so we can make carnitas?"

"Carnitas? No, mijo, we are going to sell the meat."

"What about the party?" Oscar asked.

"Party? No, there will be none of that, mijo." His father explained that he was going across the border to the United States in search of a better job. Selling the pig to the local butcher would help pay for his journey.

"You're leaving us?" Oscar asked.

His father had once been a policeman, but now he grew corn.

"There's not enough to pay the bills. And the animals eat so much of the harvest, we barely have enough for ourselves. I have no choice but to go to el otro lado, mijo. You understand?"

El otro lado—the other side.

Oscar didn't answer him.

A WEEK LATER, HIS FATHER WAS GONE. OSCAR'S MOTHER QUICKLY fell into a funk. When Oscar went to school in the morning, she sat by the woodburning stove, silent and sad. When he came home in the afternoon, she was still there, just staring into the fire. With his father gone, Oscar had no choice but to take on new responsibilities.

He fed the animals by himself, and when he ran out of hay, he went door-to-door, trying to buy alfalfa from his neighbors with the few pesos the family had. Soon, they had to sell the cows to get by. When it rained, water streamed into their home through gaping holes in the rusted roof. Oscar and his sister, Luz, placed buckets to catch the leaks.

Luckily, his father had gotten a job at a potato farm in Idaho and sent $100 a month. It was enough for the family to get by, but Oscar missed his dad. He was in fourth grade and was a star student. He placed first in the local academic competition and second in the state competition. He won a trophy—the first his school had ever gotten. The teachers showed the trophy at an assembly and even built a trophy stand to display it. But the person Oscar most wanted to admire his trophy wasn't there—his dad.

A few weeks after Oscar's eleventh birthday, his father called to say that immigration agents had come to the potato factory and arrested the workers who didn't have permission to be in the country. Now that he had been caught in the immigration raid, he was being deported from the United States. Oscar didn't know what *deported* meant. He hoped it wasn't painful.

Though he didn't understand what his father had done wrong, Oscar was excited to have his father back!

CRISTIAN

CRISTIAN WAS PUT IN A PROGRAM FOR STUDENTS LEARNING ENGLISH as a second language, but he couldn't learn fast enough. He could read all the words; he just didn't know what they meant. He got scolded when he couldn't understand an assignment. And he got bad grades.

Some of his schoolmates weren't friendly, either. Although he finally figured out how to find the right bus, there were other problems. One day on the bus home, he heard a word followed by laughter: "Wetback!" Cristian didn't know the word was a slur that originally referred to Mexicans crossing the Rio Grande into Texas, but he sensed it was an insult meant for him. The kids felt bolder on the bus because the bus driver was busy driving and couldn't do anything to stop the taunting. Cristian kept quiet.

THAT SUMMER, TEMPERATURES ROCKETED UP TO 110 DEGREES. Stanfield became an oven, and the family moved to a trailer on the outskirts of town. When Cristian went outside to play in the dirt, it burned his hands. When he grabbed a piece of metal to make something, it singed his skin and left a blister. After that, he just stayed indoors. They had a television and could sometimes pick up a broadcast of *Power Rangers* from Nogales, about a hundred miles to the south. There was a lot of static, but at least it was in Spanish!

One day, he flipped onto a show of a bearded white guy using a circular saw. The man had gray hair and sounded like he had a cold when he spoke. But what caught Cristian's attention was the saw in his hand. He was cutting through a piece of wood. Cristian quickly realized that the man was building a staircase.

His younger sister complained. "Put on the cartoons!"

But Cristian refused to let her change the channel. He had just discovered the magic of Bob Vila, home-improvement genius, and fell in love with his popular fix-up-your-home show.

In a trailer out in the middle of the Arizona desert, Cristian was blown away by Bob Vila and the machines he used. The show was in English, but even if he didn't catch every word, he understood the language of the cement mixer. He could make sense of the twisted hose of an air compressor. He loved watching the power tools and how they made the dust fly. Vila's table saw looked huge, like something a giant would use. The show was a glimpse into a magical world where people had an endless amount of building supplies and extraordinary tools. Why waste time watching cartoons? Bob Vila's *Home Again* was the real fairy tale.

It was thrilling to watch but also frustrating. The lot next to Cristian's house was filled with old cars. Untold mechanical riches were just on the other side of a chain-link fence, but the man who owned the property refused to let him check out his cars.

"You're stealing parts from me, aren't you?" the man yelled.

Being accused of stealing made Cristian angry. "Your cars are nothing but junk. Nobody wants them!" he yelled back.

Every year, he couldn't wait for the rainy season. It usually started around June. The wind would pick up and whip huge plumes of dust thousands of feet into the sky. The dust clouds blotted out the sun and made the heat more tolerable, but that wasn't the best part. What Cristian liked most was the free building supplies that would blow into his yard, from cool-looking tumbleweeds to basketballs, which he used to make models of the solar system. One day, a twelve-foot plastic swimming pool spun down out of the sky and landed in front of his house!

When there was a break in the rain, Cristian would go outside and gather his treasures.

OSCAR

WHEN HIS DAD GOT DEPORTED BACK TO MEXICO, OSCAR WAS GLAD that life in Temósachic was back to normal, but his dad wasn't happy.

"In Idaho, I can make more in one *hour* than I make here in one *day*," he said.

Oscar understood his father's frustration, but he was still shocked at hearing his father say, "I'm going back to the United States."

To make ends meet, the family had already sold their last two pigs. His father now sold their mule to a neighbor to raise money for his trip. Oscar begged him not to sell the colt, and his father agreed, but he found a buyer for the two horses. Oscar was heartbroken and burst into tears at the news.

His father took Oscar aside and told him something more terrifying. "I won't be sending money every month, mijo. I'm going to save everything I can and use the money to bring you all north. I don't want to be separated from you anymore."

"So why are you leaving us again?" Oscar asked.

"Because life is better on the other side of the border."

TO OSCAR'S RELIEF, HIS DAD KEPT HIS PROMISE OF SENDING FOR the family.

Almost everyone in his small town had traveled north to the United States at some point. One freezing December morning, it was Oscar's turn. He boarded a bus with his mother. They traveled north through the desert on Highway 17 to Agua Prieta, a dusty border town across from Douglas, Arizona. He was carsick the whole way.

Three of his dad's friends had green cards and agreed to help. They met Oscar and his mom in a little plaza in Agua Prieta. Although they had a car, they didn't want to risk smuggling anybody and getting sent to jail. So they drove around town, looking for a "coyote," a smuggler who could sneak them across the border.

They stopped at an auto-body repair shop and a tire store and finally found two guys willing to take them. They claimed to be coyotes, but they looked more like drug addicts. One was skinny and had swollen eyes. The other was very overweight. To Oscar, the man didn't seem strong enough to walk very far. They agreed to guide Oscar and his mother to the United States, but only if they got paid first.

They headed to a spot outside Agua Prieta where the border fence went from a huge twenty-foot-tall wall of iron to a thin chain-link fence. Where the two fences met, the chain link was busted open to create a six-foot hole. The coyotes told them the rules. "Keep up. Hide when you see the trucks of the US border patrol. And if we get caught, you better not tell them we are coyotes. Got it?"

They looked his mother up and down, and Oscar felt a spike of panic. It was open desert, and they were out there on their own, just him, his mother, and two strangers they'd met an hour before. Oscar knew he wouldn't be able to fight the men if they attacked his mother, but he could throw a rock hard, and his aim was good. As they set off for the edge of the fence, Oscar picked up a rock, just in case.

They squeezed through the hole in the chain link and trudged north. The sun was going down, and the skinny coyote started jogging. His mom was wearing shoes with short heels, which made it hard to walk on the uneven ground. The other coyote, already out of breath, stayed close to her. Oscar stuck by his mother's side. He was terrified of getting caught and going to jail. Or worse. His mother could get caught, and he'd be left by himself with no idea what to do. He didn't even know where the coyotes were taking them. What if they were getting them lost on purpose, leading them deeper into the desert where no one could help them?

It was dark now, and they could barely see the ground in front of them. The moon hid behind thin clouds. Oscar worried about stepping on a snake or a scorpion. The cold desert air made him shiver. It had been in the low sixties during the day, but now, with the sun gone, the temperature took a dive. He had never been so scared in his life.

After what felt like hours of walking, they arrived at a dry creek bed. A hundred feet away, a border patrol camera rotated on a post. They moved carefully past it, staying on its blind side until they came up the opposite bank and into an open field with knee-high grass. A dusty road ran through the middle of the field. The skinny coyote pointed to some large brown buildings in the distance. "That's where we're heading," he said.

They were about sixty feet from the road when the skinny coyote hissed, "Get down!"

A border patrol truck was driving up the dirt road right toward them. Through the tall grass, Oscar could see that on the back of the truck was a big cage with captured migrants trapped inside. The other coyote's head kept popping up above the yellow grass, and he refused to lie down, no matter what anyone said. As the truck went past, the agent looked at them but didn't stop.

"He must have been full," the scrawny coyote whispered. "But he probably called for backup." If they wanted to make it, they needed to run the rest of the way.

They ran and ran until they reached the back of one of the buildings.

"Our job is done," the skinny coyote told them. "Walk around to the front and go inside. You'll be picked up there." Then he and his friend disappeared into the darkness.

Oscar and his mom cautiously moved around the building and stepped into the bright lights shining on the sidewalk. They saw lots of gray-and-blue shopping carts, and a large illuminated sign above the entrance said WALMART.

They went inside and waited in the garden department—the spot where they had been told they would be picked up. Oscar felt safe among the rakes, shovels, and potted plants. He found the moist smell of the potting soil comforting and realized how exhausted he was.

Finally, his dad's friends arrived in the garden department. Oscar and his mother followed them outside to a brand-new Lincoln that smelled of leather and plastic. He fell asleep as soon as he got inside.

LORENZO

WHEN LORENZO'S GODFATHER, HUGO, CAME TO LIVE WITH HIS family, the house got more crowded. There were already too many people living there—sleeping on bunk beds, on mattresses on the floor, on the pull-out couch in the living room. But Hugo squeezed right into the family home and even set up his own little car-repair shop in their driveway. Anybody with car problems could pull in, and Hugo would pop the hood, figure out what was wrong, and fix it right there.

After school, Lorenzo started helping his godfather fix cars. Well, sort of. His godfather wouldn't let him do much more than clean the tools with a rag damp with gasoline, while his older brother, José, helped. But that meant Lorenzo could stand beside the cars and watch. He learned that when you jack up a car to work under it, you should always put a tire on the ground right next to you. That way, if the jack fails and the car drops, the tire will get squished, not you.

That's a smart idea, Lorenzo thought.

He heard his godfather explain to José that it was important to keep track of all your parts. "Anything you take off a car, remember where it goes," he said. When Hugo installed a rebuilt engine, Lorenzo stood a few feet back as his godfather showed José how to use a torque wrench to tighten the bolts. Lorenzo listened carefully and tried to get as close as he could to the car. He had to be careful, though. If he got in the way, he'd get yelled at and told to go inside.

The chief lesson Lorenzo learned was that it was important to be creative. His godfather wasn't running a normal mechanic's shop, with a wall full of tools and shelves filled with supplies. He had little money, a small set of hand tools, and his imagination. To survive, he had to come up with fresh ideas and adapt.

Lorenzo took that to heart. He didn't fit into white American culture and couldn't find his place in the immigrant community. But his days looking over his godfather's shoulder in the driveway had taught him to think outside the box. In the driveway, a strange idea wasn't necessarily bad.

Actually, it might be the *only* solution.

CRISTIAN

CRISTIAN AND HIS FAMILY MOVED TO A RUN-DOWN TRAILER PARK called Catalina Village in West Phoenix. The five-foot cinderblock wall surrounding it was covered in graffiti or painted over with random colors. Cristian read the sign at the entrance: NO LOUD MUSIC/NO MÚSICA ALTA. He saw a pair of tennis shoes hanging on electrical wires over the entrance. It was a not-so-secret signal that one could buy drugs there in the trailer park.

Still, their single-wide pink trailer felt like a huge step up to Cristian. At least there wasn't dirt everywhere. It was also just a block away from school. That meant no more school buses and no more bullying on the way home.

But now he felt sick all the time. His nose was clogged and his eyes watered. His mother took him to a doctor to get tested.

"Cristian is allergic to almost everything," the doctor declared.

"You'll have to stay indoors and watch more television," his mother said.

That was fine with Cristian. He soon found that watching Bob

Vila's show had actually taught him English. He started getting straight As. He now picked up everything so fast, he wondered why everyone else in his class was so slow. All of a sudden, school was boring to him.

He didn't meet a teacher who inspired him until eighth grade.

"Is there a project that interests you?" his chemistry teacher, Ms. Hildenbrandt, asked him.

"I want to study rocket science," he said. "I want to explore how different fin designs can affect how a rocket moves through the air."

"That's a great idea," Ms. Hildenbrandt said.

Cristian got two other students to be part of his launch team. Together they scrounged a few dollars and bought a model-rocket kit from a mail-order catalog. Then, after school one day, Cristian tied fishing line to one end of the soccer-field fence and ran the line back about 160 yards to another fence. Kids were playing a game on the field, but he ran the string down the sideline. He thought it'd be okay.

Cristian pulled the string taut and attached the rocket to it. He was excited. The experiment seemed perfectly designed. He was careful to put the smallest engine possible in the rocket; based on his calculations, the rocket wouldn't travel all the way to the other fence. He would ignite the rocket, watch it zip horizontally along the string, and measure how far it flew. By repeating the launch with different fin designs, he'd determine which fin was the most *aerodynamic*—that is, which one allowed the rocket to travel with the least resistance through the air. That was the idea anyway.

He carefully stuck the electric igniter inside the solid-fuel motor, paid out the wires, and, just for fun, started a countdown: "Three, two, one, blastoff!"

The rocket engine erupted with a roar. To Cristian's horror, the heat melted the plastic string. Now loosed from its guideline, the rocket was free to fly in any direction. It shot across the playground. The kids playing soccer in the middle of the field screamed and dived for cover.

Then, suddenly, the rocket pivoted, shot straight up into the air, and let out a huge boom above the field. A teacher came running out of a classroom and saw the terrified children scattering everywhere. Up above, the rocket was slowly coming down from the sky beneath a parachute. While everyone else kept their distance, Cristian ran excitedly toward the rocket.

"You, boy. Off to the principal's office at once!" the teacher said.

Sitting in the office, Cristian listened as the principal scolded him. "You must never do something so foolish again," the principal warned.

"I understand," Cristian said. But inside, he was already wondering what his next experiment might be.

OSCAR

OSCAR'S HOME IN THE UNITED STATES WAS A ONE-BEDROOM apartment with peeling paint, a front yard full of dirt and trash, and neighbors who blasted music all night. The apartment was tiny, and, to Oscar's disappointment, they had to share it with another family. He and his parents took the living room while the other family took the bedroom.

He was enrolled in Isaac Middle School, but he didn't speak any English and had trouble finding his way to the right classroom on time, and he ended up lost in the hallways. In his little school in Mexico, the students had stayed in the same room, and it was the teachers who moved from classroom to classroom. Not only was it confusing to navigate the hallways, but also the language barrier was a problem. To Oscar, the teachers sounded as if they were saying one long word after another. And they talked so fast! He just sat quietly and, like everyone else, said, "Hee-er," when his name was called.

Within a few weeks, however, he was beginning to get used to school, and he started to pick up a few English words. But it wasn't enough to help him make friends.

Later in the school year, the teacher asked, "Does anybody want to participate in a science fair?"

Oscar raised his hand. If nobody was going to talk to him, he might as well entertain himself.

Since he had grown up in a region of Mexico where beans were planted, he chose to study how light and humidity affect the germination of beans—the process of how the seed turns into a plant. He used a small closet at home to conduct the experiment and wrote his observations in a notebook. He surprised his teachers. Not long ago, Oscar couldn't speak the language. Now he turned in a well-written report on bean sprouts in English. His report won a $200 prize at the county science fair.

AFTER HE GRADUATED FROM MIDDLE SCHOOL, OSCAR ENROLLED AT the local high school. He walked through the school entrance on West Roosevelt, past security guards, two squad cars, and a handful of cops. A sign read, CARL HAYDEN COMMUNITY HIGH SCHOOL: THE PRIDE'S INSIDE. Once, decades ago, nearly all the students at the school had been white. Now it was mostly Latino.

Still, Oscar showed up as a freshman with no place to belong. He didn't want to feel so lost, so he tried out for the football team. It seemed like the thing to do. The problem was that he had no idea how to play the game. He was cut from the team. He tried playing soccer, but the style of play he was used to in Mexico wasn't the same in the United States, and the coach kept benching him for playing rough. Oscar felt as if nobody wanted him.

During football tryouts, he had seen a group of students jogging around the field in desert-camo T-shirts. They moved in perfect lines and made the same movements together. While the football players ran the bleachers five or six times and then collapsed in a heap at the bottom, the camo-clad students ran up and down dozens of times and never seemed to tire. Each time they got to the bottom, they dropped to the ground for a lightning-fast set of push-ups before heading back up the bleachers. It was as if they were mocking the oversize, heavily padded ballplayers.

Oscar asked around and found out that those kids belonged to the Junior Reserve Officers' Training Corps. Just like ROTC cadets on college and university campuses, high school JROTC cadets learned marksmanship, orienteering, and mountain-climbing skills. They got uniforms and had special ranks just like in the military. You could be a lieutenant, a captain, a major, or even a colonel. To Oscar's thirteen-year-old eyes, the JROTC cadets seemed like action heroes.

He signed up and got his own green uniform. Cadets had to wear the uniform on Wednesdays, and the footballers called them "pickles." Oscar got angry about their insults, but Major Glenn Goins, the group's instructor, taught him and the other cadets to not let the footballers' taunting bother them.

"The best defense is to make sure you can outrun, outclimb, outshoot, and outthink any aggressor," Major Goins said.

Oscar felt welcomed by the group. The mission of the JROTC program was to "inspire young people to become better American citizens," and though some of the cadets—like Oscar—were probably not legal citizens, they weren't turned away from the program. No other group had ever welcomed Oscar before, so when he put on his green service uniform, he felt a pride he wasn't used to.

It was nice to belong somewhere.

LORENZO

WHEN LORENZO GOT TO CARL HAYDEN COMMUNITY HIGH SCHOOL,
he decided he might try to join the marching band as a way to fit
in and make friends. To prepare him, his mother found a piano
program offered by the Salvation Army where Lorenzo got a free
upright piano that was missing some keys. His mother set it up
on the back porch so he could practice. Lorenzo taught himself
how to play pieces by Debussy ("Clair de Lune"), Erik Satie
("Gymnopédie No. 3"), and Chopin ("Sonata No. 2"). Lorenzo
could listen to the music a few times and then play it back. He
thought he was learning enough that he could wing it at band
practice, and so he joined up. He soon realized that band was not
a place where winging it worked.

The first problem was that the band had no piano. The closest
thing the music teacher could come up with was the xylophone.

Along with this large instrument, the teacher assigned him a
uniform and hat. Christmas neared and so did the annual holiday
parade. "Get ready," the teacher said.

Without any training, Lorenzo strapped the hulking xylophone to his body and marched along with the rest of the band as
they paraded down Central Avenue in downtown Phoenix. The
songs they were performing had big parts for the xylophone, but
Lorenzo couldn't read sheet music, so he had no idea what to do.
He hit a few notes with his mallets every now and then, but they
were always wrong. As the parade streamed endlessly through
downtown Phoenix, he kept wondering when the humiliation

would be over. The best he could do was keep his legs marching in time with the others.

To Lorenzo, it wasn't a parade. It was a walk of shame.

He turned in the xylophone and his uniform and never returned to band.

He felt that he didn't belong anywhere. He was desperate to find friends or at least people who wouldn't make fun of him. But it was high school, and he looked funny. Also, he had been forced to do first grade twice when he was still learning English, so now he was a year older than his classmates. Everyone always thought Lorenzo had flunked a grade and treated him as if he were dumb.

Lorenzo tried to get the kids who bothered him to be more understanding. When he mispronounced a word in English and everyone laughed, he begged for sympathy: "Why you gotta make fun of me for something I meant?" They only laughed harder. Lorenzo's anger grew, and he started picking fights at school. He ended up bruised, scraped, and in the principal's office. He was on track to being kicked out.

"I'm sending you to anger-management classes," the school counselor said.

Lorenzo learned that his anger was explosive, the most dangerous type. If he didn't control his rage, he could hurt himself or others. The counselor showed him how to calm himself by counting backward from ten. The problem was, Lorenzo wasn't sure he wanted to calm himself. It was hard to ignore all the teasing.

CRISTIAN

CARL HAYDEN COMMUNITY HIGH SCHOOL WAS ONLY SIX BLOCKS
away from Cristian's house. The neighborhood around the school
was poor and looked abandoned, with roads that were unpaved
dirt and junk-food wrappers and diapers peeking through the
weeds on the side of the road. The buildings were old and plain,
but what Cristian cared about was that his local high school
offered two interesting magnet programs: computer science and
marine science.

He signed up for all honors courses. He hoped to avoid those
he called "the idiots," who bothered the teachers, played pranks
in class, and made fun of his love of learning. Honors students
took their work more seriously and didn't cause a ruckus.

He tested out of freshman science and took sophomore biology instead. He also tried to do extra learning by reading more
about cell biology and Shakespeare online. The problem was
that the only Internet access he had at home was via a dial-up
modem. He lost connection whenever his sister wanted to use
the phone and unplugged the phone line to the computer.

"Hey!" he'd yell. "Plug it back!"

"There are others in the family who need to use the line!" his
sister snapped. "And you're just an adopted space alien my parents found beside a garbage bin."

Cristian ignored his sister. He wanted more out of life. He
wanted to have access to the world. School was dull and too easy.

He quickly became one of the top two students in his class of six hundred. But he was bored. Really, really bored.

Luckily, his life was about to change.

CRISTIAN COULD HEAR THE CARL HAYDEN MARINE-SCIENCE magnet program before he saw it. As he walked down the hallway, the thumping beat of a bass drum echoed off the linoleum tiles, and the music of a techno song vibrated through the air. The sound came from Room 2134, a dark, windowless classroom lined with fish tanks. The soft light in the fish tanks made the room almost look like a nightclub.

Cristian looked around the strange classroom and thought it was empty. He finally spotted a figure in the back, playing music off a series of computers. The man was wiry like a runner and had a beard.

"Excuse me. Are you the teacher?" Cristian asked.

The man lowered the volume and said, "Technically, I'm the program manager of the marine-science program." He came out to shake Cristian's hand, smiling and full of energy. "I'm Fredi Lajvardi, by the way. And you are?"

"I'm Cristian Arcega. I heard from my friend Michael Hanck that you can build robots here?" As he looked around, he saw partially assembled robots lying about—a chassis on one table, a circuit board on another. The room did seem like the perfect refuge for tinkerers, inventors, and frustrated dreamers. He was all of those.

"Yes, robots," Fredi Lajvardi said. "Are you interested?"

It was what Cristian had been waiting his whole life to hear.

OSCAR

THANKS TO THE JROTC, OSCAR WENT FROM BEING A SKINNY, 115-pound kid to a 140-pound dynamo. At first, he could barely do a few push-ups, and his pull-up attempts were laughable. But two years later, in his junior year, he could fire off seventy-six push-ups in a minute and do set after set of pull-ups.

He became the commander of the Adventure Training Team, the most enthusiastic group of cadets. They competed in wilderness races in which they had to haul forty pounds of water up mountains and run with backpacks filled with sand. With Oscar cheering on the team, they began to beat JROTC programs from much larger schools.

Unlike other schoolwork, which had little to do with everyday life, JROTC felt *real*. As Oscar found a place among his schoolmates, his feelings about his new home were also changing.

Oscar took pride in his Mexican heritage, but he now saw himself as an American, too. The United States had been good to him, and he wanted to show his appreciation. He was getting a free education, and his family was able to afford a home with a roof that didn't leak. Oscar believed it was his duty to give back to the United States.

"I want to enlist, sir," Oscar said to his JROTC instructor one day.

"Do you have a green card, son?" Major Goins asked.

"No, sir."

Major Goins looked at him with regret and told him that even though Oscar had everything the military was looking for—leadership, intelligence, dependability, integrity, tact, selflessness, and perseverance—it wouldn't help him reach his dream. He needed papers.

"You know, there was a time when that was okay," Major Goins said, like during World War II and the Vietnam War, when Canadians were allowed to join the US military. "But it's not gonna work anymore. You gotta be a US citizen or a legal permanent resident."

Oscar felt as if the air had been sucked out of him. He didn't know what to say. He looked at Major Goins for a moment but then snapped to attention. This was just an obstacle, nothing more, and it was the mission of a cadet to overcome all obstacles. The bigger the obstacle, the better the opportunity to prove the cadet's mettle.

"Thank you, sir," Oscar said, pushing past the flash of disappointment. As he walked away, he decided there was only one solution: to become the best cadet the program had ever seen. *Maybe if I'm good enough, something will change,* he thought. He dreamed that he would go to college, serve in the military, and go on to have a career as an engineer. What did he have to do to get there?

WHEN OSCAR WAS A JUNIOR, THE BATTALION WENT TO FORT Huachuca, an army installation near the Mexican border. Active-duty soldiers ran the teenagers through the camp's obstacle course and assigned them puzzles to solve. Oscar gave it everything he had and pushed his teammates to follow his example. Running the obstacle course, Oscar hauled people over the walls and picked up their loads if they couldn't carry them. He seemed to be everywhere at once, cheering on his teammates, zipping up ropes, and racing under low-slung webs of barbed wire.

He made an impression. Goins promoted him to cadet major, making Oscar the battalion's executive officer. He was now responsible for planning events, coordinating students, and teaching the younger cadets the basics. He also commanded the Adventure Training Team, and under his leadership, the team took on incredible physical challenges and soon became an official unit within the battalion.

At the end of Oscar's junior year, Oscar won another trophy—the JROTC Officer of the Year. At the ceremony, his green uniform was decorated with rows of ribbons for all the medals he had been awarded. A nameplate over his right pocket read VAZQUEZ. The trophy was a golden statue of a cadet standing at attention, and Oscar held it, beaming as he took a photo with Major Goins. It was one of his proudest moments.

But it wasn't enough.

Two other cadets had green cards and enlisted in the armed forces at the end of junior year. Oscar watched as they shipped out for basic training that summer while he stayed home in Phoenix, working at a mattress factory with his father.

No trophy would change the fact that his mother had taken him across the border at night without a visa.

 **LORENZO**

AFTER THE XYLOPHONE DEBACLE IN BAND, LORENZO FELT LOST. HIS cousins started a gang called WBP—for Wetback Pride. They taught Lorenzo their hand signs and let him hang out with them. It was a way of belonging to something, but he didn't want to get in trouble. He wanted something else.

Lorenzo liked his marine-science class with Fredi Lajvardi and started to hang out in the room after class. He would noodle around the fish tanks and listen to Fredi talk about building things. What captured his attention were all the tools in the closet across the hallway. There were more tools in there than his godfather had, and students were allowed to use them. But Lorenzo was used to hanging back, so he just watched as Fredi fed the fish and scrubbed the tanks over lunch.

One day, Fredi handed him the scrubber and pointed at the tanks. "You want to learn how to do this?"

Lorenzo laughed nervously. "Uh, sure." He'd never had much responsibility. His father didn't seem to have respect for him and hardly noticed him. His godfather wouldn't let him use the tools in the driveway. Now a teacher was putting the lives of his fish into Lorenzo's hands! No one had ever trusted him like that before.

Fredi showed him how much food to put in each tank and how to clean algae off the aquarium walls. Looking after the tanks quickly became part of Lorenzo's routine. When it was time to do a deeper cleaning, he came in on a Saturday to help Fredi partially drain the tanks.

"Yuck! This stinks!" some kids complained. But the smell didn't bother Lorenzo. He was used to worse. Sometimes he fished for tilapia in concrete canals that reeked of sewage. But it was a cheap meal.

After the tanks had been scrubbed, Fredi said, "Want to go to McDonald's? My treat."

Lorenzo didn't know what to say. Nobody had taken him to a restaurant before, not even for fast food. His family ate beans and rice most days. There was no extra money to spend on luxuries such as a meal out.

"Come on, kid," Fredi said, hustling Lorenzo into his Chevy Silverado truck.

At the McDonald's, Lorenzo stood nervously in line beside Fredi. He didn't know what to order and was worried that he might get something too expensive.

"What do you want?" Fredi asked.

"You go first."

"Let me have a Big Mac with fries," Fredi told the cashier.

"I'll have that, too," Lorenzo chimed in.

When they sat down, Fredi started telling Lorenzo about robotics.

"The students on the team get to use all the tools in the closet, from the hacksaws to the drills," Fredi said, taking a bite out of his Big Mac. "You can learn computer programming and mechanical engineering, both of which are skills that can help get you into college. Plus, it's fun."

Lorenzo was hooked as soon as Fredi said the words *hacksaws* and *drills*.

"I'm in," he said.

CRISTIAN

THE CARL HAYDEN ROBOTICS TEAM WAS NOT VERY POPULAR. NOT many kids even knew there *was* a robotics team at their school, so only a few had signed up. If it hadn't been for his friend Michael Hanck, Cristian wouldn't have known about it, either.

Even though he'd joined the team too late to help build a robot, Fredi said, "We're gonna build a trebuchet next. You could help us out the rest of the year."

"What's a tre-boo-shay?" he asked.

"It's a medieval gravity-operated catapult," Fredi said, as if it were the most obvious thing in the world. "We're going to fire pumpkins out of it at Halloween!"

"That sounds awesome!" It was the first time Cristian had found something at school that excited him. But he was also cautious. He was used to being let down. He tried not to get too excited.

It was hard to hold himself back. He started using his free time to hang around the marine-science lab. Fredi showed him a video of students converting a Pontiac Fiero into an electric car. The students had challenged the local police to a race at a training track and beat the cop car. They had also built an electric vehicle that looked like a Formula 1 race car. *This is cool*, Cristian thought to himself.

He had the second-highest GPA in his grade, but that wasn't the only thing that impressed his new teacher. When Fredi needed to install a batch of new computers, Cristian volunteered to set up a LAN—a local area network—so that the computers could work together. Book smarts were good, but Cristian's ability to assemble something on the fly was just as valuable.

Cristian started to see another kid hanging around the lab. His name was Lorenzo.

It wasn't Lorenzo's unusual haircut that caught Cristian's attention. It was his habit of cracking jokes and causing useless distractions. He called guys like Lorenzo "idiots."

But together with Lorenzo and Michael Hanck, Cristian helped to construct a huge catapult that could hurl pumpkins toward the horizon. This was the first time in their lives any of them had free access to power tools. So instead of designing a simple catapult that could easily be carried, Michael made a drawing of a five-hundred-pound giant that stood fifteen feet tall and rolled on four-foot-diameter wooden wheels.

"Meet the MOAT," Michael said, "aka the Mother of All Trebuchets."

"It's awesome!" Lorenzo and Cristian said.

As Cristian and his team members excitedly began to put together their huge hurling contraption, Fredi warned them to not get carried away with their fantasies.

"You boys need a leader," Fredi said.

OSCAR

BY THE START OF HIS SENIOR YEAR, OSCAR REALIZED THAT HE NEEDED to find something else to do with himself. He was disappointed that since he didn't have permission to be in the United States, he couldn't make a career in the army. He hadn't worked this hard to end up at a mattress factory like his dad. His parents had brought him to Arizona to give him a chance to accomplish more than they had been able to.

Oscar had no idea what to do now.

One October day, he walked into Fredi Lajvardi's marine-science classroom, searching for new ideas and opportunities. He was as excited as when he'd joined the JROTC. He didn't want to just *take* the class; he wanted to push himself and everyone around him to do something amazing. He liked Fredi, who had been born in Iran but grew up in Phoenix. Fredi had experienced rejection and discrimination firsthand. He was the kind of teacher who understood what immigrant kids like Oscar were going through.

"You know, Oscar," Fredi said one day, "I have a bunch of kids building a catapult in the robotics club. How do you feel about joining?"

Oscar listened closely. He liked building things and was good with power tools after many weekends and summers working with his father at the mattress factory. There he'd learned to use saws and heavy-duty staplers, to measure things and cut wood.

"Sure, I'll check it out," he said. He appreciated that Fredi was offering him a new team to lead.

He was soon impressed by what he saw. Michael Hanck's trebuchet design was under construction—a wooden tower that held up a bench-press bar fifteen feet off the ground. The bar was loaded with 120 pounds. When released, it whipped a twelve-foot two-by-four through a 180-degree arc, hurling whatever was on the end into the distance.

"Your catapult is awesome," Oscar told the guys. "But you've got a big problem."

Because the arm extended twelve feet, it required a lot of leverage to pull the 120-pound weight into firing position. Cristian would dangle off the arm, and the structure barely budged. Oscar shook his head. This bunch of skinny nerds had built a catapult so big, they would have a hard time firing it.

He felt he could solve the problem. As the commander of the Adventure Training Team, he was used to climbing rock walls and dangling from ropes. He regularly ordered his JROTC squad to crawl on each other's backs to form a pyramid. This would be no different.

"Move aside," he said. He climbed up a rope to the top of the trebuchet arm and pulled it down a little bit. Then he ordered Cristian, Lorenzo, and Michael, plus others in the club, to grab the rest of the rope and climb on. Their combined weight was enough to lower the bench-press bar into the firing position. He'd done it.

LORENZO

THE TREBUCHET WAS SCHEDULED TO HAVE ITS BIG DEBUT AT Mother Nature's Farm in Gilbert, Arizona. The local pumpkin patch hosted an annual pumpkin-hurling contest. Cash prizes and bragging rights were at stake. Lorenzo was excited. He had never hung out with seniors, let alone someone as serious and focused as Oscar. He was also impressed by Cristian's smarts. Together they had all built something twice as tall as any of them.

"We'll leave at six in the morning tomorrow," Fredi told the team the day before the contest. "The pumpkin patch is a half-hour drive, and we need time to assemble the trebuchet when we get there."

Lorenzo couldn't wait to see it in action.

But the next morning, he slept late and woke up a few minutes before six. He lived ten minutes from the school and leaped on his twenty-speed bike, hoping the team was still there. To his horror, he discovered that the rear derailleur on his bike was busted, and his chain was stuck on the smallest sprocket in back, the one he used only when racing downhill. He strained to get going, but the high gearing was tough. He could barely pedal the crank at first. Once he was on the move, he huffed and puffed his way down the predawn streets, pushing as hard as he could.

He was a block away when the school van sped right past him. He was out of breath and couldn't even yell for them to wait. He watched the van turn onto the freeway on-ramp, pulling the trebuchet on a trailer.

Disappointed, Lorenzo watched as the catapult he'd helped build sped up onto the interstate and disappeared. He was two minutes late. He was furious with himself and his lack of discipline. He'd put all that effort into the project, and now he'd messed up badly. He was supposed to be there to watch the pumpkins get hurled across the sky. It was his fault he was missing out on the fun. He went home and thought about this lesson on how not to be late.

Next time, he'd need to do better.

CRISTIAN

OUT AT THE PUMPKIN FIELD, CRISTIAN DIDN'T MISS LORENZO. HE hadn't had a lot of respect for him to begin with, and now he had even less.

"If he can't wake up on time, that's his problem," Oscar said. "Every cadet knows there's no excuse for being late."

Cristian agreed. Lorenzo had a long way to go to earn the group's trust.

The pumpkin-hurling event began, and Cristian, Oscar, and Michael Hanck struggled to arm the trebuchet. Cristian was wearing black shorts that hung below his knees with white socks pulled up his calves. He sported an oversize white T-shirt and a wispy mustache. He looked like a nerdy gangster. When it was time to pull the catapult's arm down, he watched Oscar easily climb his way up the rope. Michael pulled from the midpoint, and Cristian dangled off the rope at the bottom, his skinny legs swinging in the air. It took all three of them to get the arm into position. When they fired it, the catapult made a satisfying *whoosh* and flung the pumpkin about one hundred feet.

They added more weight to the bench-press bar the next time, and they were able to increase what they called the "rate of hurl," inching up to 150 feet. That placed them in second, behind a school from the richer part of East Phoenix.

"We gotta add more weight," they said, hoping to beat their competitors. But to their disappointment, the extra weight created so much force, it broke the trebuchet arm in half.

The boys had to content themselves with second place.

"It doesn't matter. That was fun!" they said.

What Cristian and the others learned from the experience was that it was too difficult to handle such a large, heavy machine, especially for a bunch of skinny nerds. Maybe their next project would be something smaller.

PART TWO

LUIS

LUIS ARANDA STARTED OUT AS A SIX-POUND BABY. HIS MOTHER

thought he looked like a beautiful little doll and showed him off to her friends. The family lived in a shack in Cuernavaca, in the Mexican state of Morelos. By kindergarten, Luis was one of the biggest kids in the neighborhood. And he kept getting bigger and bigger. Nobody knew why.

His mother worked as a house cleaner for a rich Japanese woman. Many days, Luis's mother would bring him to work, and the woman took a liking to him. She watched Luis as he stumbled around the property and played in the dirt. One day, she saw him hug his mom and say, "I love you, Mami."

The Japanese woman teared up. "I remember when my children used to say that to me," she said. She decided to make a startling offer. She would adopt Luis. She would take good care of him. He'd have good food to eat, nice clothes, and maybe even get to visit Japan. She would give him a world of opportunities his family couldn't afford.

His parents were struggling. Luis's father worked as a construction laborer but had left to find a job in the United States as a farmworker. His mother had gone to school only through second grade and married when she was fourteen. Now she was about to have another baby.

Yet his mom wouldn't give Luis away. She couldn't part with

him, even if it meant he would lose out on all the nice things the Japanese woman could give him. And she was determined that she would do everything she could to give Luis a better life. So, she decided she would have to take him to the United States.

She quit her job, packed a small bag, and took Luis by the hand. "We're going somewhere else," she said. Together with his grandfather, an aunt, and two cousins, the family set off for the border town of Nogales by bus. Then they walked through a hole in a chain-link fence on the border and took a taxi to Phoenix, where his dad had found work as a butcher.

AS TIME PASSED IN PHOENIX, LUIS GREW EVEN MORE. BY fourteen, he was taller than his parents, and by sixteen, he was 205 pounds and six feet tall. He was a quiet kid who liked watching life go by. He saw the world as a fun place and thought everything "small" people did was amusing.

What he didn't like was school. Reading made him sleepy. But he knew his parents had made sacrifices to bring him to the United States, and he didn't want to let them down. Also, his dad had become a legal permanent resident in the United States and was able to get green cards for Luis and his mom. That meant Luis was one of the lucky kids who didn't have to live in fear of deportation.

He went to school and tried his best.

In middle school, Luis had started washing dishes at Amici's, an Italian restaurant. By then, he had three more siblings, so there were a lot of mouths to feed. After school, he would work at the restaurant from four to ten P.M. to help his family.

Working in the kitchen was fascinating. Luis quietly watched the chefs churn out dishes he'd never seen or heard of—fettuccine Alfredo, chicken lasagna, shrimp scampi. At home, he watched cooking shows on TV and loved the way Julia Child prepared a roasted turkey.

"Can you make a dinner that way?" he asked his mom.

"I'll try," she said.

She bought a turkey, simmered it in broth, and served it with a thick mole—a rich, flavorful sauce made of more than thirty ingredients, like dried peppers, tomatillos, spices, pumpkin seeds, chocolate—the way it was done in Mexico. His mom's heart was still in Cuernavaca, and she never cooked anything that wasn't Mexican.

Luis complained, "This doesn't look like the roast-turkey dinner on TV!"

His mother cut him off. "Next time, you do it."

So Luis started cooking. In eighth grade, he roasted a turkey. "It could use some mole sauce," his mother said. But Luis was happy with his effort. Okay, so the meat *was* a little dry, sure, but it was still a classic American roast turkey.

BY THE TIME HE STARTED GOING TO CARL HAYDEN COMMUNITY

High School, Luis was working as a short-order cook at a restaurant next to a bowling alley. The pay was terrible—five dollars an hour—but for a while, making food for people was exciting. He found a better job as a dishwasher at a place called Doc's Dining & Bar. One morning when the kitchen got overwhelmed by too many customers looking for French toast and chicken-fried steaks, Luis offered to help out. His boss wasn't so sure—Luis rarely spoke, and his boss didn't know what to make of him. But when he whipped together a ham-and-cheese omelet, his boss was impressed. Luis felt proud. He knew that if you were quiet and watched, you could learn a lot.

AT THE BEGINNING OF SENIOR YEAR, LUIS ENROLLED IN FREDI'S marine-science seminar. The class was an opportunity for seniors to work on their own projects. Luis thought it'd be an easy way to get credit toward graduation. Fredi offered the seniors a bunch of possible topics—ocean currents, marine-animal migrations— but he also gave them the choice of working on robotics. Luis was pretty sure he'd fall asleep in class if he had to read any textbooks. So he said, "I'll do robotics."

It made him feel good that the team seemed to welcome his help. He didn't know Cristian or Lorenzo, but he knew Oscar— the cadet was hard to miss whenever he wore his pickle-green uniform—and they had had classes together since middle school. Now that Luis and Oscar were both seniors in Fredi's seminar, they saw each other throughout the week, and Oscar was friendly. Many people on campus were intimidated by Luis's size and silence. But Oscar wasn't scared and treated him like anyone else. He made Luis feel part of the team.

"Lo haremos juntos," he told Luis during class one day. "We can build something great."

Luis nodded and, because he was a boy of few words, simply said, "Okay."

LORENZO

"OKAY, KIDS, LISTEN UP. I'VE GOT NEWS FOR YOU," FREDI SAID TO THE team one day. "We are entering the MATE Robotics Competition sponsored by NASA and the US Navy!" The Marine Advanced Technology Education Center, Fredi said, was hosting a new robotics competition at the University of California. The center's mission was to encourage students to explore careers in marine technology. The competition was a fun way to get kids excited about ocean work.

This would be the Carl Hayden team's first time competing in an underwater-robotics event.

"Here's the mission statement," Dr. Cameron, the other science teacher, said, handing the boys a twenty-two-page short story about the destruction of *U-157*, a U-boat that had been torpedoed in the Caribbean in 1942. During the contest, students would explore a mock-up—that is, a life-size model—of the submarine in a swimming pool. The story was meant to fire their imaginations.

"I want you to read it at home," Fredi said.

Lorenzo read the story in his bedroom. There were funny-sounding German words and something about a secret agent. Eventually, the German submarine is destroyed by a mysterious explosion off the coast of Florida. The captain is then miraculously rescued by a Spanish-speaking fisherman named Pedro Sánchez.

"Whoa, whoa, whoa," Lorenzo said to himself. Submarines, explosions—all that was fine. But the mention of Pedro Sánchez caught his attention.

The next day in class, Lorenzo had a question for Fredi: "So a Mexican saved the captain's life?"

"I don't know if he's Mexican," Fredi said. "He's probably Cuban, since it's Florida."

"They'll probably say the Mexican was the one who sank the sub and put him in jail," Lorenzo joked.

"Okay, enough of that. Focus on building the robot," Fredi said. "Let's go through the mission." He ticked off the required tasks. The competition was set to take place at the campus in Santa Barbara, California. The model of the submarine would be in one of the university's pools. The contestants had to build an ROV—remotely operated vehicle—that could dive down to the replica submarine and complete the following seven tasks:

- **Measure the submarine's length**
- **Calculate its depth**

- **Navigate inside the submarine to recover the captain's bell**
- **Recover a lost piece of research equipment**
- **Recover a sonar device that would be lying on the pool bottom**
- **Sample liquid out of the secret-cargo barrels**
- **Take the temperature of water seeping out of a cold-water spring**

Lorenzo laughed. "There is no way we can do any of that!"

"Yeah, I'm not so sure we can, either," Cristian said.

Luis just looked blankly at the others without saying anything.

Only Oscar was enthusiastic. "Come on, guys. We can do this! We just have to start working on it."

"We live in the desert," Lorenzo said. "We don't even have a pool to practice in."

"We can talk to Scuba Sciences," Fredi said. As a marine-science magnet program, the high school offered scuba certification through Scuba Sciences, a local dive shop with an indoor pool that was twelve feet deep. "I bet they'd let us come in."

Lorenzo wasn't convinced. Fredi and Dr. Cameron glanced at each other. It seemed both teachers were also afraid that the boys might not be able to handle the challenge.

"Look, we appreciate your enthusiasm, Oscar," Fredi said. "But this *will* be a difficult project."

It was a problem. The organizers of the ROV competition promised it would be very technically challenging. Lorenzo could tell that the last thing either teacher wanted was to make the boys feel bad about themselves. The whole point was to give them a chance to accomplish something beyond what they thought possible. But if they showed up at the event and completely failed, it would only make them feel that they didn't belong in the contest in the first place. That would just make Lorenzo forever feel like he wasn't good enough.

"Well, what's the worst that can happen, that you guys build a robot that will simply sink to the bottom of the pool and short out?" Fredi asked.

"At least we'll finally get out of Arizona," Lorenzo said.

"It'll be fun to go to Santa Barbara and check out the event," Cristian said. They'd get to see how other, more sophisticated teams worked together. They'd learn a lot and be able to apply the lessons to future years.

"We sure about this?" Dr. Cameron asked.

The competition would be split into two classes: Ranger and Explorer. The Ranger class was geared toward high school teams; the Explorer class was aimed at colleges.

"The Explorer class is for teams that are willing to make an advanced, multifunctional ROV. The control and payload system has to be really sophisticated," Fredi said as he read the competition overview. "The robots will need a higher power limit and are usually costly to build."

But even the Ranger division sounded intimidating to Lorenzo.

"The Ranger class is for high school students," Fredi continued reading. "But don't be fooled. The Ranger-class mission tasks are just as challenging as the Explorer class."

As Fredi read the names of the high schools that had competed in the first two competitions, he saw that a college had competed at the high school level.

"Wait a second," Fredi said, an idea forming. "If colleges can enter the high school division, that means high schools can enter the college division, right?"

"MIT is in that division," Dr. Cameron pointed out.

The boys were at a real disadvantage, but at least they had a choice of whom they could lose to. "So what do you say, guys? Would you rather get beat by a bunch of high schoolers or by MIT?" Fredi asked them.

"Who's MIT?" Oscar said. None of the boys had heard of the university.

"The Massachusetts Institute of Technology. It's the best engineering school in the country," Dr. Cameron said. "Maybe even the world."

"It's basically a school filled with Cristians," Fredi said, looking at Cristian.

"So it's, like, a school for *dorks*?" Lorenzo joked.

"Shut up," Cristian snapped.

Luis watched in silence, a grin on his face.

"You want us to go up against the best school in the country?" Oscar asked.

"We want you to have a good time and learn a lot," Fredi said.

"And if you're in the mix with MIT, you'll probably learn more than you would from lesser teams."

"I'm not going to enter something to lose," Oscar said.

"Then let's work hard and build a great robot," Dr. Cameron said.

"What are our chances of doing well?" Oscar asked.

"We can aim to not finish last," Fredi said. "That'll be a good goal."

Lorenzo giggled. "That can be our motto: 'Don't finish last.'"

OSCAR

THE IDEA OF FINISHING LAST DIDN'T SIT WELL WITH OSCAR. AT THE team's first design meeting, he took charge. "We're gonna kick butt, okay?"

Lorenzo laughed until Oscar's stare shut him up. Oscar started going over the description of the contest. MATE's official introduction to the Explorer-class mission began with a quotation from General George S. Patton: "Accept the challenges so that you may feel the exhilaration of victory."

Oscar liked that. He was ready, even if the others weren't, and he was determined to drag them along with him.

The third paragraph of the mission statement also made an impact: *This is an exploration mission. Exploration means discovery of the new—and the unexpected. This competition will push your imagination and technical skills. Enter the event with the spirit of the men and women explorers who have set out into the unknown.* The words were meaningful to Oscar.

"First things first," he said. "Let's figure out how we are going to pay for it all. MATE will cover meals and housing in Santa Barbara and will give us one hundred dollars for building supplies. That's barely enough to cover the cost of driving to California. We're going to need a lot more than that."

Fredi suggested they try to drum up donations. He printed brochures about their team and the competition for the boys to give to people when they asked for support.

"What are you talking about?" Lorenzo said. "You want us to ask people for money? I don't know anybody with money."

"Ask your family," Fredi said.

Lorenzo laughed. "They don't got nothing."

Oscar looked at his friends. He knew it was going to be hard for all of them.

AFTER SCHOOL, OSCAR STOPPED BY QUALITY BEDDING, THE mattress factory where his father worked. Since Oscar also worked there sometimes on weekends and summer breaks assembling box frames alongside his dad, he knew the owner and many of the workers.

He handed a brochure to the owner and said, "West Phoenix is going up against the best of the best! But we need local support so we can have a shot. Can you help?"

His boss read over the brochure, impressed that Oscar was participating in a NASA-sponsored underwater-robotics contest.

"And you can write off your donation on your taxes," Oscar told her. "We can give you a receipt."

To his shock, she wrote a check for $400, and one of his dad's coworkers chipped in another $400!

Oscar was really proud of himself.

CRISTIAN

CRISTIAN DIDN'T HAVE THE SAME LUCK AS OSCAR. HIS PARENTS couldn't spare any money, so he phoned uncles and aunts in California and southern Arizona. They said they'd think about it but never sent in anything.

At the team's next meeting, Cristian learned that Lorenzo hadn't had any luck with his family, either. "When I told them I'm going to be competing in an underwater-robotics competition, they thought I was joking," Lorenzo said.

Luis handed them a check for $100.

"Where you get that from?" Cristian asked, surprised.

"My boss," Luis said shyly. The owner of the restaurant where he worked had chipped in.

"So we have nine hundred dollars," Oscar said.

Cristian had a lot of respect for Oscar, and now he had even more.

"Woo-hoo, we're rich!" the boys said. Little did they know that some of their competitors had more than $10,000 in their budget.

Now that they had some funds, the team could get serious about building their remotely operated vehicle. They started by breaking apart the trebuchet they'd made for the pumpkin-hurling contest. They wanted to reuse some of the pieces to figure out how big their robot needed to be in order to fit propellers, sensors, and controls. After taking apart the giant slingshot, they used the two-by-one lumber to make a simple box structure to approximate the dimensions of their ROV. Once it was done, they stood around the awkward wooden model in the robotics closet and talked through the tasks they were going to have to complete.

"Okay, so first, we have to measure the depth and length of the submarine," Cristian said. "How are we going to do that?"

"How about a length of string?" Lorenzo said. "We can keep it simple. The ROV can stretch the string from one end to the other; then we can measure it. We can also lower the string until it touches the bottom of the pool and get a depth reading that way."

It did not seem like a good idea to Cristian. "And what if it doesn't reach the bottom?" he pointed out.

Lorenzo thought about it for a second. "Yeah, that's a problem."

The group continued brainstorming. After a minute, Lorenzo came up with a new approach. "Hey, what if we hung a string down from a floating thing? We could draw markings on it every foot and use a camera to see how far down it went."

Cristian thought about it, then shot down the idea. "The string could get caught in the propellers. And we're punished if we leave anything behind in the pool, so we'd waste time trying to pick it up."

Lorenzo looked disappointed.

"But it wasn't a terrible idea," Cristian said, trying to make his teammate feel better.

Lorenzo brightened. "What about just using a tape measure? We can tie a loop onto the end, hook it onto the submarine, and drive the robot backward. The tape will just spool out."

"How do we read it?" Oscar asked.

"Aim a camera at it," Lorenzo said. "We can read it off the video monitor."

"That could work," Oscar said.

Lorenzo looked so proud of his idea, Cristian hated being the one to question it. "It won't work for depth, though," he pointed out. "There's nothing at the bottom of the pool to hook on to. So how are we going to measure how deep it is?"

They decided that they'd need two solutions. Lorenzo's tape measure would work for the sub's length, but they'd need something else to get the depth. They talked about using a scuba-diving computer—they might be able to borrow one from the dive shop—but its margin of error was too big for the exact measurements they were required to make.

"What about a laser tape measure?" Oscar asked. Besides working at the mattress factory, he sometimes did construction work hanging drywall, and he'd paid attention to how the plumbing and electrical wiring was done. "I worked with my brother on a construction site and saw the workers using this cool device that could tell you the distance just by aiming a laser beam at an object."

"Will it work underwater?" Cristian asked.

"I don't know," Oscar said. "I've never used one."

"You guys should call somebody," Fredi advised. "The best way to figure something out is to call an expert."

Cristian felt he could figure it out on his own, given time. But what if he couldn't? Or what if he took too long to do it? Time was precious.

"I'll make the calls," Oscar said.

OSCAR

BEFORE CALLING ANYONE, OSCAR STARTED BY GOOGLING "LASER tape measures" and quickly came across a company called Distagage in Marathon, Florida. The company specialized in lasers that could read distances as far as 330 feet with an accuracy of an eighth of an inch. Some of the lasers could even measure the slope and length of a roof from the ground. The website noted that their top-of-the-line devices were "used by more construction professionals around the world than any other brand."

"Sounds expensive," Lorenzo said.

He was right. They sold for $375 to $725 each. It seemed

pointless to even consider them, but Fredi encouraged Oscar to call anyway. "Just ask for advice," Fredi said.

"Distagage, this is Greg De Tray speaking," the voice on the phone said. "How can I help you?"

Oscar was nervous talking to this stranger, but he took a deep breath and jumped right in. "Hello, sir, my name is Oscar. I'm part of the Carl Hayden High School robotics team in Phoenix, Arizona. We are building a remotely operated vehicle to compete in a competition sponsored by NASA, and we need to measure depth underwater. We were thinking about buying a laser tape measure from Home Depot and wonder if you had any advice?"

"Those are useless," De Tray said. "They aren't real laser finders. The laser is only good to show where the thing is pointed at." He said that the actual range finding was done *acoustically*—meaning, by sound waves—and the measurements were usually wrong. "Those so-called laser range finders give the whole industry a bad name. So definitely don't get one of those."

"Do your range finders work underwater, sir?" Oscar asked.

"They don't work underwater. They will give you the wrong answer, but they give you the *same* wrong answer every time. It's always about thirty percent off."

"The index of refraction!" Cristian blurted.

Everybody turned to look at him.

"What is that?" Lorenzo asked.

"The laser light is traveling through water, which has a different density than air," Cristian said.

Lorenzo Santillán in the lab at Carl Hayden Community High School.

When they met, Luis Aranda (left) was a quiet student, while Oscar Vazquez (right) was a standout cadet in the Junior Reserve Officers' Training Corps.

Cristian Arcega shows his mother the robot he helped build for the Arizona FIRST (For Inspiration and Recognition of Science and Technology) Robotics regional competition.

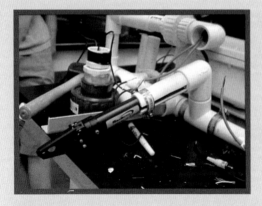

Stinky the ROV under development. Here, the black robotic grabber has been installed, and the main color camera has been wired before being attached to the frame.

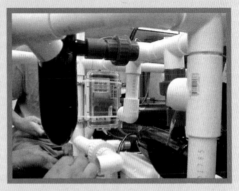

Mounted upside down in a watertight clear plastic case, the laser tape measure's helium-neon laser could be aimed directly underneath the ROV. A camera mount directly opposite the tape measure's screen is visible here, awaiting installation of a camera lens. Stinky's four black-and-white cameras enabled remote views of the various instruments.

This side view of Stinky offers a look at the final positioning of four of its five thrusters, used to enable movement in any direction. These electric trolling motors were operated by three remote joysticks connected to the ROV by wires in the tether.

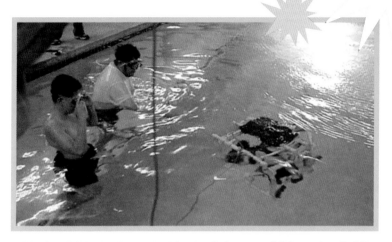

Testing Stinky in the pool at Scuba Sciences with its tether held in the foreground. To reduce the weight of the tether—which is connected to the ROV via the control system in the black waterproof briefcase on top—one set of video wires was used to switch between the four black-and-white cameras on Stinky's frame. The main color camera used its own set of video wires.

The color monitor shows the view directly in front of Stinky in the Scuba Sciences pool, with two of the three thruster-control joysticks visible. The other monitor is switched by a control pad between the four black-and-white camera views of the various instruments. The pad also has switches for the pump and grabber. Here, the grabber is being engaged.

A fuzzy view of Stinky in the process of being painted.

The milk-jug nest used to support a balloon that will be attached to the black pump nozzle to gather liquid during the competition.

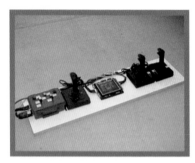

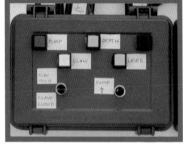

The remote-control setup, with a close-up view of the control pad.

From left: Oscar, Luis, Lorenzo, Allan, Cristian, and Fredi with Stinky outside of Scuba Sciences before the competition.

Photos of "Stinky" Con't.

Open Pelican Case housing the control system and also acts as buoyancy.

Custom made fittings to bring electrical wires to the Pelican Case from pvc frame

Color CCD camera housed in 1/2 a pcv union. O-ring seal visible with lexan cover off.

Camera with cover on, as well as the two microphones (red film canisters) and the claw.

Camera aimed at laser distance meter. Also rov battery in yellow Pelican case.

Rear view of rov with angled horizontal thrusters for greater steering.

An excerpt from the 21-page tech report prepared by the team for the judges at the competition. The full report can be viewed at https://images.macmillan.com/folio-assets/discussion-guides/9780374388614DG.pdf.

From left: Lorenzo, Oscar, Luis, and Cristian in June 2004 at the Marine Advanced Technology Education ROV Competition in Santa Barbara, California.

The university pool with an underwater obstacle platform.

Some of Stinky's competitors.

The Carl Hayden Falcon Robotics team at work during the competition.

Posing and celebrating after the awards ceremony.

Lorenzo and Luis gave Cristian a blank stare, but Oscar thought he understood.

"I get it," Oscar said. "Water is harder to move through than air."

"Things move slower," Cristian said. "Because water is heavier than air."

"So if we take thirty percent off the readings, it'll give us the right measurement," Oscar concluded.

"Exactly," Cristian said.

They may have solved the refraction problem, but De Tray's devices still cost hundreds of dollars. How could they ever pay for it?

"Sir, sorry, you still there?" Oscar asked De Tray.

"Yeah. You know, I'm impressed with you kids," De Tray said over the phone. "I tell you what. You guys want to use my range finder on your robot, I'll send you one. You can borrow it."

Oscar looked at his friends. They had never thought that random strangers would be interested in helping them. Oscar felt a surge of gratitude. He had faith in humanity, though it had been put to the test when the army turned him down. This was a sign that things were looking up. He realized that there were adults out there who truly wanted kids like him and his teammates to succeed.

"Thank you, sir," Oscar managed to say, trying to keep his emotions in check. "We really appreciate it."

LORENZO

LORENZO RARELY DID HIS HOMEWORK. HE DIDN'T SEE THE POINT.
It seemed like meaningless busywork to him. He usually earned
Cs and Ds and had a GPA of 2.08 at the start of his sophomore
year. But he wasn't too worried. He was having more fun learning
about robots than he was in his classes. Yet, a part of him hated to
admit that all the time he was spending in the robotics closet was
distracting him from his regular schoolwork. He cringed when
his geometry grade dropped to an F.

When he went to the next meeting, Fredi said, "Lorenzo, can
I talk to you about your grades?" Fredi could see student grades
on the school network and tracked those of the members of the
robotics team. "You know I'm going to have to kick you off the
team if you don't get your GPA up."

"What?" Lorenzo asked, surprised.

"I'll give you till the end of the semester, but if you're not passing all your classes by then, you're off the team."

"For real?"

"For real."

To Lorenzo, Fredi was a father figure, and he didn't want to
disappoint him. His own father didn't care whether Lorenzo went
to school or not.

"How do I pass my classes?" he asked.

"Do the homework. And sit in the front row. You'll learn more,"
Fredi suggested.

Lorenzo decided to start studying. He wasn't going to risk

getting kicked off the team. So he moved up to the front row in geometry class and began asking the teacher questions. When the homework stumped him, he would bring the workbook to the robotics closet and ask Cristian for the answer.

"No way," Cristian said. "I'll show you how to do it, but you have to figure out the answer for yourself."

Cristian wasn't a great teacher. He didn't have a lot of patience when it came to teaching things he already understood. But Lorenzo worked hard and picked it up quickly. To Cristian's surprise—and to his teammates' relief—Lorenzo started getting As on geometry tests, and his GPA began to climb.

That meant he could stay on the team—the only place where he felt that he belonged.

OSCAR

NOW THAT OSCAR HAD HELPED THE TEAM FIGURE OUT THE FIRST task—measuring the depth of the pool—he had to help figure out the next task. They had to take the temperature of a cold-water spring at the bottom of the pool. To find the spring, contestants were instructed to "look for signs of low-velocity, upward-moving currents."

Right. As if that's easy to do underwater, Oscar thought.

Once the spring was located, the ROV had to put a sensor into the stream of cold water and report back the temperature.

They weren't going to be able to hover in place for long, so they needed a thermometer that could quickly take the correct measurements.

Oscar tracked down a supplier in Stamford, Connecticut, that specialized in temperature measuring. But the supplier, Omega Engineering, had more than a hundred thousand products, including strange-sounding instruments such as the "general-purpose air velocity transducer" ($882) and an "electromagnetic flow meter" ($2,500). It was hard to make sense of it all, so Oscar dialed the company's 800 number.

"May I speak to someone about thermometers, please?" he asked.

The operator connected him to Frank Swankoski, a temperature engineer at the company. Oscar put on the speakerphone so that Cristian, Lorenzo, and Luis could listen in, too. The team huddled around the phone.

"Hello, sir," Oscar said when the man answered. "I'm calling to get some advice on how to build a complex underwater robot."

"Are you calling about the national underwater-ROV championships?" Mr. Swankoski asked.

"That's right, sir. You've heard of it?" Oscar asked, surprised.

"Yeah. A few weeks ago, some college oceanic-engineering students called and said they were entering the competition."

Oscar looked at his friends and knew that, like him, they felt disappointed at hearing that other teams were making the same phone calls. How could Carl Hayden beat them?

"My high school team in Phoenix is competing, too, sir," Oscar said. "We're going up against colleges like MIT, and we need to learn as much as we can from experts like you. We don't know exactly how best to measure temperature underwater, and we would appreciate your advice."

Oscar almost expected the man to hang up. Why would he want to talk to a seventeen-year-old kid from an unheard-of high school when he'd just spoken to college students?

To his surprise, Mr. Swankoski launched into an in-depth explanation of the supplies the company sold, offering details as if he were letting Oscar and his teammates in on a little secret. "What you really want," he confided, "is a thermocouple with a cold-junction compensator."

Thermocouple? Cold-junction compensator? To Oscar, that sounded like a foreign language. He didn't want to admit he didn't know what the man was talking about, but fortunately, Mr. Swankoski explained.

He ran through the science. You take two alloys—a metal made by combining different metallic materials—and put them side by side. The alloys have different abilities to conduct energy, and when put near each other, they transform temperature into voltage. That's a thermocouple. When an alloy is attached to a thermometer, another alloy can be placed outside the device to sense the temperature around it. The amount of voltage generated between the alloys is a sign of how much temperature difference there is. The data can then be used to figure out the outside temperature.

"Whoa," Lorenzo said. "That's awesome."

"How much does the device cost?" Oscar asked. His stomach hurt just thinking about the price.

But Mr. Swankoski surprised him. "I'll donate one," he said. "You know, I think you can beat those guys from MIT. Because none of them knows what I know about thermometers."

After they hung up, Oscar looked at Lorenzo, Cristian, and Luis and wanted to jump up and down. But he didn't. He had to be cool. "You hear that?" he said to the guys. "We got people believing in us, so now we got to believe in ourselves."

IN NOVEMBER, A FEW WEEKS AFTER THE TEAM STARTED THE ROV project, Luis got in the van with five of his marine-science classmates, and Fredi drove them west. "If I'm going to teach you kids about the ocean, I better show you the thing," Fredi said.

Luis ended up sitting with Oscar and felt self-conscious about taking up too much room.

He knew that Oscar and the others didn't know him well. His large size and blank gaze made people stay away. He was the quietest kid on the team, and he usually faded into the background. But now he was going to sit here in the van with Oscar for five hours, so he decided to strike up a conversation about Oscar's car, which he'd noticed him driving.

"Hey, I really like your car, man," Luis told Oscar.

"Thanks," Oscar said. He explained how he'd saved money working at the mattress factory to buy his 1991 Mitsubishi 3000GT, a two-door sports car.

"What do you drive?" Oscar asked.

"An '89 Camaro RS."

It was a serious American muscle car, meant for racing, and Luis loved it. He'd saved the money he made at the restaurant.

"Get out of here!" Oscar said, impressed.

Feeling more comfortable with the conversation, Luis started talking about his car's attributes—it had a cherry-red paint job and a 3.05-liter V-8 engine. He spoke in a gentle voice. He'd always been a shy kid, but Oscar made him feel at ease, and Luis stopped being shy. He talked all the way to San Diego.

THE OCEAN WAS MIND-BOGGLING TO LUIS. HE AND OSCAR HAD glimpsed it on a previous school trip to California. But neither of them had ever been in it. Now they dived into the water and couldn't believe how salty it was. They were used to freshwater lakes and rivers.

Fredi had arranged for the students to tour SeaBotix, a San Diego–based ROV manufacturer. Luis marveled at the facility. The place was a dream. Racks held specially designed mechanical grippers, endless spools of wire and cable, and beautifully molded plastic casings for robots.

They were given a tour of the laboratory by the company's president, Donald Rodocker, who was a legend in the ROV community.

He wore a neatly trimmed gray goatee, round spectacles, and a green plaid shirt.

"Hey, kids, I want you to meet my latest vehicle," he said.

Luis stared at an amazingly compact orange robot called the LBV, which stood for "little benthic vehicle."

"It can dive five hundred feet and cruise at 2.3 miles per hour underwater," Rodocker said.

Luis was shocked to learn that the base model sold for more than $10,000, and the price went up with add-ons.

Despite its tiny size, the robot still had the same problems larger ROVs had: its tether—that is, the data and control and power cables it is tied to. Once in the water, an ROV is connected to the surface by a bundle of cables that allows the person operating it to control the propellers, sensors, and manipulators. The cables also carry video and infrared signals so that the operator can see where the ROV is going. Normally, the tether also powers the robot.

Luis learned that a major engineering challenge was to make those cables smaller without making the ROVs move slower from getting less power. Another problem was that the tether could get caught on something, and the ROV might not be able to get free.

While Rodocker talked about building advanced ROVs, Luis saw Oscar leaning in close to the LBV. Its arm sticking out the front had a claw that could grab different objects. He guessed Oscar was thinking that it would be the perfect tool to complete three of their mission tasks: recovering the U-boat captain's bell and retrieving the lost research equipment and sonar device.

Rodocker noticed Oscar's interest. He talked about the many models they'd built of the claw until it operated correctly. "It took a lot of work to make something that was small and highly functional," he said.

Luis had questions, though he was too shy to ask anything. But Oscar didn't have a problem asking his. "Sir, would you consider lending us one of your early models of the claw if you aren't using it anymore?"

"I'd be happy to," Rodocker responded easily.

Luis and Oscar looked at each other and smiled. *Score!*

ON THE DRIVE BACK TO PHOENIX, LUIS AND HIS CLASSMATES couldn't believe their good fortune. Loaded in the back of the van, they had a state-of-the-art model of a claw on loan from a real ROV company. For that reason alone, the trip had been a great success.

But there were other things that Luis was grateful for—his first taste of the ocean and his friendship with Oscar.

But then a problem appeared in the heat waves coming off the I-10. Near Yuma, Arizona, just after they left California, they spotted brake lights. Cars were coming to a stop. A row of official vehicles bore the logo of US Immigration and Customs Enforcement. The students were headed into an immigration checkpoint.

Luis had a green card thanks to his father, but he knew that Oscar was in the country illegally. He could be arrested and deported.

"Give me your school IDs," Fredi commanded. "And nobody talk besides me. Understood?"

The kids nodded and nervously handed their IDs forward. Fredi eased up to the checkpoint and rolled down his window. An officer asked for identification. Fredi handed over the school IDs. "We're on a school trip," he said.

The agent glanced at the van—it bore the school's name. Luis saw the agent looking at them, a group of Latino kids. He could sense that Oscar was terrified, preparing for the worst. Luis felt bad for his friend. What if he was torn from his family and dropped across the border?

The agent looked at the IDs and then back at the kids. After a moment, he returned the IDs.

"Okay, have a good trip," he said, and waved them on.

Fredi stepped on the gas before the guy could change his mind. Nobody talked for a while. Luis no longer had the taste of the Pacific surf in his mouth. Now it was the taste of fear. Their desire to see the ocean and learn about robots seemed foolish and maybe even reckless.

OSCAR RETURNED TO THE ROBOTICS CLOSET WITH MIXED EMOTIONS.
The anxiety he'd felt at the immigration checkpoint had gone away, but the threat was still there. He had to decide. The ROV

contest was back in California. If he wanted to compete, he'd have to risk another checkpoint. He could lose everything.

He made a quick decision. In JROTC, he had done multiple rope-climbing courses, ascending and descending sheer cliffs. He'd learned to not let his fear control him. This was no different. If he wanted to do something great, he'd have to put his worries aside. They now had a thermocouple, a range finder, and a scary-looking black claw that only an engineer could love. Oscar picked up the components and placed them in the wooden model of their robot.

"I think we can fit everything," he told himself.

With that, he put the checkpoint behind him.

SOON, CRISTIAN AND LORENZO SHOWED UP TO THE ROBOTICS CLOSET, and the team brainstormed about how to build the real ROV. Fredi and Dr. Cameron knew that other teams had used machined metal in previous years. Some colleges had their own machine shops and could custom-fabricate parts. Machined-metal ROVs tended to be smaller and more compact, which came in handy when exploring tight underwater spaces.

Oscar knew that his high school couldn't afford the metal that would be needed. They also didn't have access to a machine shop. Even if they did, nobody knew how to use the machines.

"We should use glass syntactic flotation foam," Cristian said excitedly. "It's got a really high compressive strength. They use it on submersibles."

"What's a *submersible*?" Lorenzo asked.

"Haven't you watched James Cameron's *Ghosts of the Abyss*? It's a documentary about the director's journey twelve thousand feet down to visit the wreck of the *Titanic*. The film crew used two ROVs outfitted with glass syntactic foam to enter the wreck. It's got glass microballoons embedded in an epoxy resin, so it keeps its shape under pressure while still providing buoyancy," Cristian said.

"Dude, how did you come up with all *that*?" Lorenzo said.

Cristian shrugged. "I've been looking into it."

"How much is it?" Oscar asked. Cristian could speak his fancy science language, but none of that mattered if they didn't have the money to pay for it.

"Two, maybe three thousand for what we need," Cristian answered.

"¿Qué, qué?" Lorenzo blurted. "¿Cuánto?"

Oscar sighed. Cristian always had his head in the clouds, and his ideas were not based on reality. They didn't have that kind of money, and Cristian knew it. They all knew it. They had received $100 from MATE for building supplies and had $900 in donations. Glass syntactic foam was not an option.

One option was PVC, or polyvinyl chloride, pipe. It was a material they were all familiar with from seeing it used in the fields to water the crops. The white plastic tubing wasn't as strong as metal, but it was easy to work with. It was also all they could afford.

"We can run wires through the pipe to keep them dry," Lorenzo said. "And the air inside will make it float."

"Let's try it," Oscar said.

Luis drove to Home Depot and bought twenty dollars' worth of three-inch-diameter Schedule 40 PVC pipes. When they gathered around the ten-foot-long pipes in the robotics closet, it seemed like a lot of material.

"There'll be a lot of air in there," Oscar pointed out.

Cristian started scribbling on a piece of paper and made a crude sketch of an ROV. While the others watched, he calculated the volume of air inside the pipes. "We will need some ballast," he said.

"You mean like something heavy?" Lorenzo asked.

"Yeah," Cristian said impatiently, as if it were obvious what ballast was.

The simplest solution was to attach weights to the frame of the ROV to counterbalance the *buoyancy*—that is, its ability to float. But weights would take up precious space in a machine already cluttered with sensors, propellers, and a claw. The machine would turn into a huge, uncontrollable monster. To make things worse, they would have to worry about the thick, heavy tether cable sprouting out the top.

"Wait," Cristian said, thinking for a moment. "What if we put the battery on board?"

It was a bold idea. Most teams wouldn't consider putting their power supply in the water. A small leak could take the whole system down. But the competition required agile movements through narrow passages; a thinner tether would be a key advantage.

"We can put the battery in a heavy, waterproof case at the bottom of the ROV, where it would stabilize the machine's movements," Cristian said. "It will make sure the robot has all the power it needs and serve as ballast. If the battery is right next to the propellers, we won't have to worry about them not having enough juice, and we wouldn't need to run a thick electrical cable to the robot from the surface."

"What do you think?" Oscar asked the group.

"That's a badass idea," Lorenzo said, his highest compliment.

Oscar was worried, though. "There's a reason other people don't do it."

"If we do the same as everyone else, we'll finish last because they've done it before," Cristian fired back.

"If our ROV short-circuits, we'll definitely finish last," Oscar said.

"Sure, but if we can't figure out how to completely waterproof a battery case, then we shouldn't be in an underwater contest," Cristian said.

"He's got a point," Luis said abruptly.

Everybody looked at him.

Luis looked calmly back at everyone else.

Oscar had even forgotten he was there. Because Luis hardly ever talked, Oscar knew he had to pay careful attention to his teammate's words.

"Okay, then," Oscar said. "Let's put the battery on the robot."

LORENZO

FOR LORENZO, THE ROBOTICS TEAM WAS LIKE A NEW FAMILY.
He saw his mentors Fredi and Dr. Cameron as an extra set of parents. They gave him advice. They pushed him to do better. It was the same for the others. There was a growing sense of camaraderie and team spirit.

Lorenzo wasn't the only one sitting in the front row of his classes. The rest of the team did it, too.

"What's the point of doing something halfway?" Fredi told them repeatedly. Lorenzo and the others took that to heart.

The team wasn't a perfect family, though. Lorenzo felt that Cristian criticized his ideas too much. Oscar saw Lorenzo as someone he couldn't count on. Luis showed little emotion of any kind, so Lorenzo couldn't tell where he stood with the big guy.

On the positive side, the team at least listened to Lorenzo and let him dream up crazy ideas. They didn't make fun of his appearance. The robotics closet felt more like home than his actual house. Lorenzo would have been happy living in the cramped classroom.

But that wasn't possible. He stayed as late as he could after school, but both Fredi and Dr. Cameron had a forty-five-minute drive back to their families in East Phoenix. Lorenzo usually hung around until Fredi shut off the lights and started locking the doors. With a sigh, Lorenzo would then head home.

Fridays were the hardest. That's when Lorenzo's dad would start drinking, and Fredi and Dr. Cameron weren't always able to come back to school over the weekend. That meant two days of hell, getting tormented by his dad.

The tension at home made it harder for him to handle the abuse at school. The rest of the students still teased him about his appearance. He wanted to look cool and started wearing jewelry: two gold earrings in his left ear, a gold chain with a medallion, and a flashy metal watch. But as he passed people in the hall, they still laughed. He was a walking joke to them.

The taunting got worse when he started sophomore year. One day, in public-health class, a kid behind him started teasing him about his hair.

"You look like a girl!" he heard the guy say. "Doesn't he look like a girl?" he asked his friends.

Lorenzo ignored the guy. A minute later, he felt something hit the back of his head. The guy had flicked a wad of gum into Lorenzo's long hair. Lorenzo tried to pull it out, but the gum got more and more stuck. Everyone burst out laughing. He was so ashamed. He had gum stuck on his fingers and in his hair, and the laughter of his classmates echoed in his ears.

When he got home that night, he burst into tears.

"I'll cut out the gum, mijo. Don't worry," his mother said.

"No!" Lorenzo said between sobs. He wasn't going to cut it. No way was he going to give that guy the satisfaction of seeing his hair ruined. His mother grabbed some vegetable oil and started trying to loosen the gum. She eventually got it out.

"Gracias, mama," Lorenzo said, and hugged her.

Soon after the gum incident, Lorenzo was trailed home by

another student. As he crossed over the Thirty-Fifth Avenue overpass, the student started asking Lorenzo why he was wearing earrings and a flashy watch. Lorenzo ignored him for a while, but the kid kept pestering him. Lorenzo finally stopped and turned.

"This is how I am, okay?" he said.

"But you look stupid," the kid said.

Lorenzo tried using his anger-management techniques. "Diez, nueve, ocho, siete . . . ," he counted backward. He knew that if he got in another fight, he could be kicked out of school. Before, he might not have cared. Now he wanted to build this robot and stay on the team.

The kid behind him didn't let up. He started saying things about Lorenzo's mom, and Lorenzo tensed. How dare that kid insult his mother?

He hurled himself at the boy and landed a few punches. The kid smacked him in the face, and his fist crashed into Lorenzo's eye. Traffic on the bridge came to a halt as drivers got out and stopped the fight.

When he got home, his dad noticed his swollen eye. "Who hit you?" he asked. Lorenzo didn't want to say. "Tell me and I'll kick his butt," his father said.

It was the most his father had offered to do for him in a long time. Lorenzo felt a swirl of emotion. He didn't want to get into fights, but this was the first time he felt his dad actually noticed him. Maybe if he got into more fights, his dad would pay more attention to him. His dad didn't seem to care about Lorenzo's interest in robotics. He thought it was a waste of time.

Lorenzo wondered if he was pretending to be something he wasn't. He was just an undocumented immigrant and a violent freak. Who was he kidding thinking he could be more than that?

NEWS OF THE FIGHT SPREAD AROUND SCHOOL THE NEXT DAY, AND HE was called into the principal's office.

"You were warned not to fight again," Principal Ybarra said. "I now have a reason to expel you."

Lorenzo didn't know what to say. He felt so lost. "I'm sorry" was his only reply.

He felt the principal looking at him, as if trying to figure out what to do with him. Lorenzo didn't want to beg to be allowed to stay. But he wished he could explain himself and say why he'd acted the way he had. But he couldn't get the words out, and he braced himself for the worst. He couldn't imagine what his life would be like if he were kicked out of Carl Hayden High School and couldn't be part of the team anymore. He looked down at the floor and sighed.

"Tell you what, Lorenzo," Principal Ybarra said. "I'm going to take a chance and allow you to stay. But you have to go back to anger-management courses. This is your last opportunity. Got it?"

FREDI TRACKED LORENZO DOWN BETWEEN CLASSES LATER THAT day. "Come with me," Fredi said sternly. Lorenzo followed him back to the robotics closet.

"You've got to stop this," Fredi told him when they got there.

"What was I supposed to do? He was insulting my mother."

"You know, I got beat up in high school, too," Fredi said, "for being Iranian."

"For real?" Lorenzo couldn't imagine someone like Fredi being attacked. But when Fredi was in high school, he'd been riding his bike back home from cross-country practice when a truck full of teenagers roared up and started yelling, *"Damn Iranian!"* Their truck got so close to him, Fredi got pushed onto the curb, flew off his bike, and landed on the pavement. The teenagers kicked him hard, leaving him in a ball on the ground.

"They want you to get angry. So, if you give that to them, they win," Fredi said. "Next time somebody wants to fight you, pretend you're having a seizure." He pretended he was having a seizure, twisting and shaking violently. "Like this."

Lorenzo broke into a smile. The image of his teacher squirming on the floor to get out of a beating made Lorenzo giggle. He usually felt like the oddest person in the room, but now Fredi turned out to be a bigger goofball.

"You gotta do something, right?" Fredi asked.

The humor helped take a weight off Lorenzo. It was true that getting into a fistfight had gotten his father to notice him, but that just wasn't who he was. Unlike his dad, who was encouraging Lorenzo to fight more, Fredi was giving him a different option—to be clever and have a sense of humor about things.

"I'm serious," Fredi said. "Just flop around on the ground like a fish. They'll leave you alone."

"Okay. I'll do that," Lorenzo said. He burst out laughing. It felt good. And at that moment, he accepted who he was: a goofy kid with goofy ideas that somehow made perfect sense in the world of robotics.

FEELING RELIEVED THAT HE WASN'T GOING TO GET KICKED OUT OF school, Lorenzo returned to the robotics workshop and started experimenting, letting his imagination take flight.

He wanted to figure out how to approach the competition's third task, which was going to be the hardest. According to the fictional backstory made up by the contest's administrators, the submarine sank while it was carrying thirteen mysterious barrels. Those barrels were leaking and posed an "environmental danger" that needed to be quickly assessed. During the competition, the teams would have to find a barrel and take out a five-hundred-milliliter sample of the liquid inside it. All this had to be done with the ROV hovering underwater.

"That seems impossible," Cristian said. "You figure it out," he told Lorenzo. If he failed, they felt it wouldn't set them back much, since it probably wasn't doable in the first place.

So while the rest of the team focused on the easier tasks, they left the hard one to him. Lorenzo was fine with that.

He knew he had to think outside the box.

Keep it simple, he told himself. *Where can our team store the liquid that has to be sucked out of the barrels?* He closed his eyes, and an idea began to form in his head. He wondered if they could use a balloon.

Unlike a plastic container, a balloon carried no air when deflated, so it wouldn't add buoyancy. A balloon was flexible, could expand and contract easily, and cost almost nothing. Why make it more complicated? Lorenzo was sure he'd found the perfect container.

Fredi thought his nutty idea had potential.

The next problem was how to suction the liquid into the balloon.

"How about a sump pump?" Fredi suggested. He explained that it was a kind of pump often installed in basements where moisture is a problem. As water collects in a basin installed in the floor, a pump, often submerged in the basin, kicks on to discharge the water. So Fredi knew that a submersible sump pump would be engineered to work completely underwater.

On a mission to Home Depot, he and Lorenzo found exactly what they needed: a small twelve-volt pump for thirty-five dollars. Lorenzo also picked up some narrow copper tubing for two dollars.

Back in the robotics closet, he glued the copper tube to the pump and bent the front end so that it jutted out from the bot like the proboscis of a butterfly.

He pulled a balloon over the other end of the pump. When he plugged it in, the pump sucked up five hundred milliliters of water in twenty seconds. It worked perfectly—except that the weight of the water made the balloon fall over. This wouldn't be a problem underwater—the balloon wouldn't fall over below the surface—but when the ROV was pulled out to retrieve the sample, the balloon would flop to the side, slip off the pump, and spill the sample everywhere.

Lorenzo tried attaching the balloon in different ways, but each time, the balloon fell over and water gushed everywhere. Lorenzo had to keep sopping up the mess. It was getting a little embarrassing. Maybe the balloon hadn't been a great idea after all.

"You're doing good," Fredi reassured him. "Keep trying. You're getting close."

Lorenzo nodded. He wasn't sure he was getting close to anything but a wet pair of shoes, but Fredi's words made him feel a little better.

"Maybe if I built something to catch it, that could help," Lorenzo said.

"Try it," Fredi said.

Lorenzo fished an empty Coca-Cola liter bottle out of the garbage and hacksawed it in half. He flipped the top half upside down and placed it over the pump so that it served as a sort of catcher's mitt for the balloon. Now the balloon filled inside the container, which supported it so it didn't flop around and fall over, but the liter bottle was too restricting. As the balloon expanded, it bulged out of the top of the bottle and pulled the balloon off the pump. Water sprayed everywhere.

"Try something bigger than a Coke bottle," Fredi suggested while Lorenzo glowered. "You're onto something good."

The next day, Lorenzo showed up with an empty gallon-size plastic milk container. He cut it in half, attached it to the pump, and turned the system on for twenty seconds. The balloon filled with water and gently leaned over into the molded interior of the milk jug. Lorenzo turned off the pump. The balloon lolled inside the jug like a baseball in a glove, its bottom securely fastened around the pump.

"You did it," Fredi said, clapping him on the shoulder.

Lorenzo sat back and smiled. "I did it."

OSCAR

OSCAR AND LUIS TOOK ON THE PROBLEM OF WHAT PROPELLERS

to use on their aquatic machine. Part of the challenge was to figure out how many were needed and how best to arrange them. They couldn't be enormously powerful. The more power the motors used, the quicker they would run down the onboard battery. Another requirement was that the propellers would need to be able to guide the ROV not just forward and backward but also up and down.

"Three motors should be enough," Oscar said. "Two horizontal to drive and one vertical to go up and down."

"What if we need to tilt to pick something up?" Luis rumbled.

"You're right."

The more they talked the problem through, the more complex they realized it was.

"The robot needs to be able to tip forward so the claw can pick up the captain's bell," Oscar said.

"And to move sideways, it needs another motor," Luis said.

Mobility in every direction was critical.

"I think we need five motors total," Oscar said.

"How about electric trolling motors?" Fredi said. "Fishing boats use them to move slowly and quietly and not scare off the fish. They are efficient and small enough to fit inside the PVC frame."

Oscar googled "trolling motors" and found a company called Mercury Marine. Using the phone on Fredi's desk in the marine-science classroom, Oscar dialed the 800 number and got ahold of Kevin Luebke, one of the company's endorsement managers.

"No, sir, we aren't fishermen," Oscar explained. "We are high school students competing in an underwater-robotics contest."

"Sounds like a fun contest," Luebke said. "The MotorGuide motors sell for one hundred dollars."

Oscar scratched his head. They needed five motors, and that would cost $500 and leave them with almost nothing. "Well, sir. You see, we have a very small budget."

"I see," Luebke said. "Tell you what, I'll let you have them for seventy-five dollars each."

Oscar quickly did the math. At a total of $375, it was still a big part of the project's budget, but they needed reliable motors to move the robot around the U-boat submarine. "Thank you, sir. We'll take five."

When the motors arrived in the mail, Oscar and Luis eagerly pulled them out of the box. It was like getting a Christmas present and made the project feel even more real. They were shiny and black, and each had a propeller with two menacing blades.

The next question was how to arrange them. At Fredi's suggestion, Oscar and Luis filled a marine-science sink with water and plopped in a small piece of wood. They took turns pushing it around the sink with their fingers and discovered that if they pushed with their fingers at a 45-degree angle, they were able to turn the wood much faster than if they simply pushed it directly from behind.

Based on their small-scale sink experiment, they needed to design a robot that would be able to rotate around a central point with little drift.

"Well, now that our money is almost gone, we can't build a waterproof housing for the robot's control," Oscar said.

Instead, they found a plastic briefcase for sale at a local electronics store. It wasn't exactly waterproof, but it claimed to be water *resistant* and was advertised as being able to keep documents dry as long as it wasn't submerged for too long or deeper than fifty feet. Plus, it was on sale for $120, a bargain.

"Hey, the pool in Santa Barbara isn't deeper than fifteen feet," Cristian said. "It'll be okay."

They bought the case, drilled a hole in the side for the wires, temporarily plugged it, and dunked the whole thing in one of the marine-science room's big sinks. It worked fine, at least in a sink.

LUIS

LUIS WATCHED AS CRISTIAN DREW A DETAILED PLAN OF THE ROV, including the lengths of every piece of three-inch-diameter PVC pipe that was needed. But the pipe was sold in lengths of ten feet, so it would need to be cut into pieces. They bought a cheap pipe cutter, but when Cristian tried, all he did was make a scratch. The thick pipe was too big for the flimsy tool, and he wasn't strong enough.

Luis tried not to laugh as he watched the smaller guy huff and puff to no effect.

"Con ganas," Lorenzo teased him good-naturedly. "Squeeze that thing."

"You try it," Cristian shot back, and handed him the cutter.

"Deja te enseño," Lorenzo said, happy to show him how it was done.

Lorenzo clamped down on the tool. He could barely budge it. He tried sitting on it.

"That's not gonna count!" said Cristian.

Lorenzo banged it against a wall.

"Don't mess up the wall!" Fredi shouted from across the room.

Lorenzo succeeded in breaking through the pipe by straining with every ounce of his strength.

"See, I told you it was hard," Cristian said.

"Let me try that." Oscar took the cutter from Lorenzo. Luis watched him from across the room with a grin. Squeezing as hard as he could, Oscar cut one piece but only after working on it for five minutes. He could do it—just barely.

"Dudes, my hands hurt," he said. He looked at the pipes—they had to be cut into eighty pieces! No way could he do that.

Luis squirmed when everyone turned to look at him.

"You want to give this a try?" Oscar asked.

"Okay," he said simply.

He took the cutter from Oscar, fed a piece of pipe into the device, and clamped down. Then he sliced through the pipe in one smooth movement. Everybody looked at him with awe.

"It's like butter," he said.

"It's all yours, man," Oscar said.

It took Luis two days to cut all the pieces. As he sliced through pipe after pipe, he felt better and better. Finally, he was contributing something to the team.

As he worked, Oscar, Lorenzo, and Cristian started temporarily joining the sections together to make sure they all fit. Luis did his best to measure the pieces before he cut them, but it was hard to be exact with a hand-powered slicer. Once he was done, they placed the last piece into position and stood back to take a look at their creation.

It was a slightly lopsided white plastic frame.

"That looks good," Dr. Cameron said.

"Very cool," Fredi agreed.

Luis knew it looked terrible, but there was potential.

CRISTIAN

THERE WERE TEN WEEKS LEFT UNTIL THE ROV CHAMPIONSHIP.
Cristian and the others set about assembling their underwater
vehicle. They took a controller from another robot to use it as the
brains of their ROV. The controller was a black square that contained all the processors, connections, and radio controls needed.

Now it was time for them to learn to solder wires together
and into circuit boards. They used a solder gun, an electric tool
whose tip heats to around 700 degrees and melts a lead and tin-
based alloy to create a conductive "glue" between metal wires.
Fredi and Dr. Cameron showed them all their soldering tricks.
It took a few practice sessions with the tool, but Cristian and his
teammates soon learned to forge basic connections. Next, they
would have to connect the propellers and cameras to the controller. Cristian soon realized that there was a big difference between
soldering a connection and building an entire robot.

"We're going to practice until we can do this without thinking," Oscar said.

It was time to put the robot together, and once the PVC pipes
were glued in place, it would be difficult, if not impossible, to
make changes. They would have one chance to glue it all together,
and it had to be right.

Cristian could tell that Oscar wanted the process to move like
a finely tuned military operation. The guy took his army obsession to another level. Cristian thought of the "Be all you can be"
army motto. Oscar believed that with all his heart.

Under Oscar's supervision, Cristian and the team assembled the robot frame without glue, dry-fitting pieces together. The trick was this: The glue would dry immediately, so they needed to know exactly what they were doing with each piece of pipe before they glued it. And there were eighty pieces, so it was a lot to memorize.

They took apart the robot and put it back together over and over again. Cristian was getting frustrated, but he didn't complain. He wouldn't put it past Oscar to punish him by making him do a hundred push-ups or another similar torture.

"Again!" Oscar shouted. They took the robot apart and put it back together again. "Again!" Each time, they finished at the top, leaving enough room for the black briefcase. "Again!" At first, they made a lot of mistakes, putting a piece in the wrong place or putting it in backward, but as they practiced, they got better, until they were able to do it without mistakes.

As he looked at his friends, Cristian felt sad. The school year was coming to an end, and both Oscar and Luis would be graduating just before the competition in Santa Barbara. Once they glued the robot together and completed the competition, their high school time together would be over. They were all getting older and needed to figure out what they would do with their lives. But Cristian wondered what kind of choices they had.

He dreamed of going to college, but he might not be able to. He was a little jealous of Luis. He had a green card and more opportunities. But Cristian—just like Oscar and Lorenzo—was in the country without permission. Once high school was over and they were out in the real world, they would have to fend for themselves, with no Fredi, no team, and no robot, just them fighting alone for a chance at the American Dream.

OSCAR

GRADUATION CAME FASTER THAN OSCAR HAD EXPECTED. AND instead of celebrating, Oscar felt a deep gloom settle over him. It still hurt that the army didn't want him.

No matter how many push-ups he did or how fast he ran, he couldn't erase the fact that he was seen as a trespasser, living in the country without permission and denied his military dreams. Not only had he no chance to make a career in the army, he had no chance to make a career anywhere else.

He had little hope of being able to go to college. He wanted to major in aerospace engineering and go on to have a career building rockets. But it was just a fantasy. The best he could hope for was to be an underpaid construction worker and try to find enough steady work.

It was hard to imagine building a life on such a shaky foundation.

Still, he reminded himself that just graduating was an accomplishment. It meant a lot to his family. His parents didn't have high school diplomas, so Oscar was making history.

With that in mind, Oscar threw on his graduation gown, put the cap on his head, and paraded up onto the stage to accept his diploma. He was happy to share the stage with Luis. He knew that just like him, Luis was also the first in his family to graduate from high school. So when the ceremony was over, he gave his friend a big hug.

"We did it, man!"

"Yeah, Oscar. I guess so," Luis replied.

They posed for photos and smiled happily. His parents were really proud of him. "Felicidades, mijo," they said. Oscar's sister baked a cake. Luis's mom made birria, a spicy beef-and-pork stew. It was a simple celebration, but it was special. Oscar knew that his accomplishment would someday help the next generation in his family go even further.

WITH GRADUATION BEHIND THEM AND THE CONTEST ONLY A FEW weeks away, it was time to glue the robot together.

They had practiced assembling the plastic pipes for weeks under Oscar's supervision. Now that practice would be put to use.

"Okay, guys, here's the moment we've all been waiting for," Oscar said to the team.

As the guys laid the pieces out on a table in the robotics closet, Oscar opened a metal container of Christy's Red Hot Blue Glue. The special PVC cement didn't actually need to be heated. Oscar just dipped a brush into the container and coated it with a blob of the bright blue paste.

"Whoa," Lorenzo said, getting a whiff of the stuff. It smelled like heavy-duty paint thinner. Right away, the little robotics closet reeked of dizzying fumes.

They decided not to place a fan near the door. It might make the glue dry faster, and they didn't want it to harden while they were in the middle of placing a pipe. But soon the vapors in the closet got thicker and thicker, and Oscar's head felt like it was spinning.

He and the others ran outside to the hallway and gulped down the fresh air.

"It was hard enough remembering where each of the pieces fit," Cristian said. "Now we have to do it all dizzy and shaky?"

Oscar thought about it. "Okay, let's try this. We can take turns. We'll take a deep breath, glue as many pieces as we can, and then run out."

He broke them into teams. He and Luis would go first.

"Come on," he said, leading the way. While Luis held the first two pieces of PVC together, Oscar swabbed some of the blue glue onto each of the parts being connected. He was holding his breath, but the fumes stung his eyes. Even the tiniest breath made him dizzy. He got a few pieces set in place and then headed for the door.

Luis just smiled. "I'm okay. Send Cristian in."

Cristian sprinted in with his shirt pulled up over his nose and glued more pieces, while Luis continued to hold everything together with an increasingly large grin. Cristian looked like a manic elf, scurrying around the room with glowing white pipes.

Oscar was worried about Luis inhaling too much of the toxic vapor. Sure enough, from the doorway, he saw the big guy starting to sway like a tree about to crash to the ground.

Oscar rushed in and grabbed him. "Hey, you've got to get out of here." Oscar pulled him from the room.

Luis couldn't stop smiling.

"Are you okay?" Oscar asked.

"Yes," was all Luis could say.

Oscar looked at Lorenzo. "Your turn."

Lorenzo zipped into the room and quickly assembled a series of pieces with Cristian. The glue dried immediately when two pieces of pipe were pressed together, so they had to focus. One mis-glued portion could endanger the whole robot frame—especially as they got further into the assembly. It was like doing a large jigsaw puzzle with a lack of oxygen and pieces that froze in place wherever you first put them. After sixty seconds, Cristian started to black out. He stumbled into the hall, gasping for air.

"Damn, that's *stinky*," Lorenzo wheezed, trailing behind Cristian.

It took almost two hours to put the whole thing together amid the overpowering stench. The next step was for Oscar and his teammates to work together to fit the four legs into position. He felt a wave of nausea but tried to ignore it. Finally, they lowered the black briefcase into place. It was the crowning touch, the moment when the robot was complete . . . but there was a problem. The three pipes for the wires leading into the case didn't line up. They angled up, as if the briefcase were much bigger, creating gaps that would flood with water, shorting the entire system and sinking the robot.

"I thought you promised this would work," Cristian said to Oscar.

They had practiced everything but the briefcase placement. Oscar was furious with himself. He should have tried to fit the briefcase in when they were doing the dry runs. He'd really messed up this time.

"We have to start over," Cristian said.

The excitement Oscar had felt about building the robot disappeared. He thought he'd done a good job leading his team, and now it felt like a defeat.

Lorenzo went into the room and walked around the robot frame, looking at the pipes that were supposed to attach to the briefcase. "They aren't off by much," he said. "What if we just bend the pipe by making it hot and pliable?" Lorenzo said when he came out into the hallway.

"How?" Oscar asked.

"The electric heat gun."

The electric heat gun was a sort of superpowered blow-dryer that pumped out air heated up to 1,000 degrees. Normally it was used to dry paint, but Lorenzo remembered that it got hot enough to make paint peel off a surface.

"Try it," Oscar said.

Lorenzo dug it out of a cabinet in the robotics closet, plugged it in, and aimed it at one of the off-angle pipes. He flipped the switch and blasted the pipe with scorching air while Luis put pressure on it with a piece of metal. At first, nothing happened. Then the PVC weakened and started to bend.

"It's working!" Lorenzo shouted.

Luis pushed the pipe into position, and Lorenzo flipped off the heat gun. In a moment, the PVC hardened into the exact position where it needed to be.

"That was a pretty good idea," Oscar said. Lorenzo's imagination truly amazed him.

"Go ahead, amigo," Lorenzo said. "You can say I'm a genius."

The boys broke into laughter. They turned to look at the ROV in admiration.

"It needs a name," Lorenzo said.

Oscar remembered Lorenzo's words while choking on the glue fumes and said, "Why don't we call it Stinky?"

LUIS

IT WAS TIME FOR THE ROV'S FIRST UNDERWATER TEST. THE TEAM had arranged to visit the local dive shop when nobody else would be using their training pool. Fredi drove them in the van to Scuba Sciences, located about eight miles north of the school on North Black Canyon Highway. Luis pushed the cart that Stinky sat on and rolled it into the Scuba Sciences building.

"Thank you for allowing us to use the pool," Oscar said to Tina Lowe, an employee.

"My pleasure," Lowe said. "Let me show you where to go."

Inside the building was a store that sold scuba gear and, in the back, a forty-by-twenty-four-foot saltwater swimming pool.

It took them about an hour to lay out their gear. Fredi settled into a comfortable chair and watched the boys work. When he was younger, his parents had not thought much about his interest in robotics. Building useless "toys" wasn't going to get him ahead in life, they said. And when he became a teacher, his mother said, "You're breaking your father's heart being a teacher." They wanted him to be a doctor like them. But now, watching his students test out their robot made Fredi realize how much he loved his job.

The boys had two old computer monitors they had found in a dusty school-district storeroom and four video-game joysticks from Radio Shack. They attached the tether and connected the monitors to the robot's electronics. When they plugged everything in and turned on the power, the monitors filled with wobbly images from the robot's twenty-seven-dollar black-and-white cameras. They jiggled the joysticks, and the propellers made a nice whirring noise as they spun. Luis felt as if Stinky were coming to life.

Cristian was in charge of the joystick connected to the trolling motor that controlled up and down movements. Michael Hanck, the skinny white kid who had designed the pumpkin-hurling trebuchet, was there to help pilot the robot. He took the two joysticks that moved the robot forward, backward, left, and right. He hadn't come to the team meetings much because of his bad grades.

Lorenzo was in charge of the sensor controls. He was responsible for the claw, the cameras, and his water-sampling pump. He did a final check on them and gave a thumbs-up: "I'm good."

Luis's job was to lift the machine into the pool.

"Remember, don't grab the pipes leading into the briefcase," Oscar warned as he pulled off his shirt and slipped into the water. "Any pressure could crack the seals and create leaks."

The robot looked like a twisted knot of white pipes, so it was hard for Luis to see which tube led where. He dipped his big hands into the guts of the machine and hefted Stinky into the air. Stinky touched the water for the first time and drifted on the surface. It floated nicely.

"Stinky's baptized!" Lorenzo shouted.

Oscar grabbed hold of the robot and pulled down, but it wouldn't sink. It just bobbed around like a cork. Luis tried shoving down from the edge; Stinky refused to sink. It was as if it didn't want to be an underwater robot.

"There's too much air inside Stinky's pipes," Cristian said. Thinking that Stinky might be too heavy and sink, the team had tied on a couple of capped pipes with air trapped inside to help the robot float. But they clearly didn't need the extra lift, so they removed one pipe. Stinky still floated. They took off the second pipe, and Stinky sank to the bottom of the pool.

First it floated too much, and now it sank all the way down.

Lorenzo found a thinner piece of PVC, capped the ends so that air was trapped inside, and tied it to the robot. It worked: Stinky now had perfect neutral buoyancy. It hovered at whatever depth it was placed at.

Now they had another problem. Stinky hovered, but it tilted forward as if a strong wind were blowing from behind. When they turned on the propellers, it tilted even more. It looked like a duck with its tail up in the air and its head in the water. They needed something to lift up Stinky's nose.

Lorenzo pulled an empty bottle of St. Ives sunscreen out of a trash can by the pool. "What about this?"

"Garbage?" Oscar asked.

"It's got air inside."

"True." Oscar shrugged. "It might work."

Luis thought the robot was just getting uglier and uglier by the day. But as far as he knew, they were going to be judged only by how their robot worked.

Lorenzo zip-tied the sealed sunscreen bottle to the front of the robot, and they lowered Stinky back into the water. This time, Stinky hovered perfectly upright and level. Oscar asked Luis to grab the Hula-Hoop leaning against a wall beside the pool and throw it to him in the water. Scuba students getting used to all their equipment learned to swim through the plastic hoops. Now it was Stinky's turn.

"See if you can drive through it," Oscar told Cristian and Michael.

Michael pressed forward on the controls while Cristian made Stinky dive. The robot zoomed forward, darting through the hoop at high speed. Luis watched on the monitors as the robot zipped through the circle.

"That was badass," Lorenzo muttered beside them.

Cristian and Michael stayed focused. The robot's tether was now threaded through the hoop. They turned the robot around and tried to go back through in order to pull the tether out. It was a tricky move. Cristian tried to get the robot up in the water, but Stinky began to spin out of control. Michael tried to steer to the left, and the robot turned suddenly toward the wall of the pool.

"Watch out!" Oscar shouted.

With a resounding *thud*, Stinky collided with the wall.

"Are you having trouble seeing where you're going?" Fredi asked.

"Yes," Cristian said. "The walls of the pool are white and hard to make out via the video feed."

"If it hits too hard, we'll crack the PVC," Luis warned.

"He's right," Oscar said. "You've got to be more careful."

Cristian and Michael tried piloting the ROV through the hoop again. Just before they reached it, the robot veered off as if it had a mind of its own and slammed into the wall a second time.

Stinky's electronics stopped responding. It floated to the surface.

Fredi suggested the boys call it a day. If there was a leak that had caused the electronics to short out, they would have to fix it back at the lab.

Everyone was quiet when Luis fished the robot out of the water.

CRISTIAN

LUCKILY, A LEAK WASN'T THE PROBLEM. WHEN HE HAD TIME TO examine Stinky back in the robotics closet, Cristian checked every single connection inside the briefcase. Some of the tiny pulse-width-modulation cables—known as PWM cables—connecting the joysticks to the ROV controller had gotten loose and caused the robot to behave unpredictably during its pool test. The final bump had caused them to disconnect completely.

The team had gotten the wires off another club robot and used them for Stinky. It saved some money but also meant they were dealing with recycled cables. The only other PWM wires they had were eight feet long. It wasn't an ideal replacement—the unneeded length would clutter the cramped briefcase—but it was the best they could do. Cristian coiled the long wire inside the case and made the connections. When he powered the system on again, the joysticks seemed to work fine.

"We also need to change the acceleration curve," Cristian said to his nervous teammates. The slightest touch on the joystick sent Stinky flying. That needed to be fixed, so Cristian worked with Dr. Cameron to reprogram the ROV's software.

"Something's got to be done about its looks," Lorenzo said.

Cristian agreed with his friend. Stinky was a bit rough around the edges. But the robot was being judged on what it could *do*, not on how pretty it looked.

He watched Lorenzo examine Stinky. The blue PVC glue had dripped down the joints, leaving messy blue streaks across the robot's white plastic framing. It looked as if the machine were bleeding blue blood from every hole.

"This robot is ugly as hell," Lorenzo declared.

"What do you want to do about it, then?" Cristian said. He knew they weren't going to get any work done until Lorenzo gave Stinky a makeover.

"I have an idea." Lorenzo pulled red, blue, and yellow paint out of a cupboard in the robotics closet.

He applied red paint to any section that Luis should avoid grabbing: the tubes leading into the briefcase and the delicate camera housings.

He painted the ROV's corners yellow so the operators could better see the outside limits of the robot's frame underwater. Cristian nodded. It would help with steering.

Lorenzo colored the rest blue and told Luis to grab only the blue parts.

"Okay," Luis said simply.

In the past, Cristian had criticized Lorenzo's ideas as too dreamy or off-the-wall. But now he knew his creative teammate had proven his smarts once again.

OSCAR

A WEEK LATER, OSCAR AND THE TEAM RETURNED TO SCUBA SCIENCES.
The competition was seven days away, and he was going to drill the team with the same rigor he had drilled the JROTC cadets.

He hoped things went better this time than on Stinky's first practice run.

Oscar had put together a list of all the tasks in the competition from easy to hard. The easiest ones that scored the highest points would get done first. He got a clipboard and barked orders like the captain of a ship.

"Everyone, ready for the first task?" Oscar shouted. The guys nodded. "Okay, go!"

This time, Cristian and Michael steered clear of the walls, and Stinky responded better to the joystick. It also correctly measured the twelve-foot depth with the laser range finder. The mechanical claw did well grabbing a piece of PVC pipe from the bottom of the pool. And the tape measure was able to capture the correct length of the pool.

After watching the team run through all the other activities they would have to do in the contest, Oscar arrived at the last task on his list: Lorenzo's balloon challenge. The liquid sampling proved to be the most difficult task. The small copper suction pipe was too hard to position. During the competition, they would have to insert the pipe into a half-inch hole. They tried practicing with a piece of three-quarter-inch PVC tube, but they couldn't get the copper pipe into the larger hole. The team knew the pump worked just fine and could suck up five hundred milliliters of water in twenty seconds. But Stinky just couldn't get into the right position to extract the liquid. To Oscar, that task seemed hopeless.

If they could do everything else, maybe it wouldn't matter.

One thing was for sure: Stinky zipped around the pool with ease. Just for fun, Fredi got in the water, grabbed on to the robot, and got dragged around the pool. The trolling motors were small but powerful. Michael and Cristian worked well together, and over their two sessions driving the robot, they'd learned how to steer in coordination. By the end of the practice, Oscar felt a surge of confidence.

"Nice work, team!" he said as everyone exchanged high fives.

"WE GOT BAD NEWS," FREDI SAID THE DAY BEFORE THEIR DEPARTURE. "Michael won't be coming to Santa Barbara." They were gathered around the narrow table in the robotics closet. The fumes were long gone, so it wasn't toxic to hang out in the room anymore, but the mood was grim.

"What? Why?" Oscar asked. He looked at the other boys in shock. They couldn't lose a team member now!

"We told him he needed at least a B in summer school in order to travel to Santa Barbara, and he didn't keep up his grades. So he isn't allowed to compete," Fredi said.

Oscar shook his head. The team had less than twenty-four hours until their departure, and they had just lost one of their two drivers. Now what?

Cristian couldn't drive the robot by himself because there were three joysticks. He didn't have enough hands. Lorenzo had already figured out how to operate all the sensors, and Luis was needed by the edge of the pool to manage the tether and lift the robot. There was only one choice.

"I'll do it," Oscar said. "I'll figure out how to drive Stinky. We'll be fine." He needed to be strong for his team. Show them confidence, even if he knew it was a setback.

Fredi called Tina Lowe and asked if the pool was available for another practice session. Classes were booked, but she agreed to give them as much time as she could between sessions. They packed Stinky, raced over to Scuba Sciences, and started setting up while scuba-diving students emerged dripping from the pool and plodded past.

"Okay, you've got forty-five minutes till the next class," Lowe told them.

Oscar was quick to take charge. "Let's do this," he said.

Luis lowered Stinky into the water, and Oscar grabbed the two joysticks that controlled the robot's horizontal movements.

"Since we changed the acceleration algorithm, you can push the joystick forward a bit, and it won't take off," Cristian coached him. Oscar tapped the joystick, and Stinky responded by cruising forward—right into a wall. They could hear the deep *thud* of the impact.

"Slow down," Cristian said worriedly.

After reversing away from the pool wall, Oscar eased Stinky ahead while Cristian goosed his joystick forward, causing the robot to descend. So far, so good.

"Let's try tilting forward now," Cristian said. To pick up objects, they had to be able to tilt an inch forward. Cristian gave the robot a quick hit of upward acceleration, tilting the whole bot forward. Oscar juiced the controls, and Stinky nearly did a somersault.

"That's too much power," Cristian chided.

"I know," Oscar snapped. If he didn't get it right, they were going to lose, and it would be his fault.

"Let's just try cruising around," Cristian suggested. "Until you get the hang of it."

They did a number of laps around the pool, and Oscar was able to avoid the walls. Right when he felt he might be getting the hang of it, Lowe walked out into the pool area. "I'm afraid that's all the time I can give you and your sea monster, fellas."

LUIS

ON THE DAY BEFORE THE COMPETITION, LUIS RUBBED THE SLEEP from his eyes and drove over to the school. It was the team's travel day. They were meeting at the Carl Hayden parking lot at four A.M. It was dark out. The streets were empty.

Dr. Cameron and Fredi arrived and unlocked the marine-science building. Soon, Oscar and Cristian arrived, but no Lorenzo. Oscar looked at his watch. It was exactly four.

"He better not skip out like he did at the pumpkin-hurling event," Oscar said.

Luis hadn't been on the team then, but ever since he met Lorenzo, he'd known him to be dependable. If the team had a meeting after school, Lorenzo was always there. When Fredi told Lorenzo to improve his grades, he had studied hard and raised his geometry grade from an F to a B+. He had sworn that he'd never be late again, and the team now trusted him. More than that, they needed him.

"There he is," Oscar said with relief as Lorenzo jogged up, holding his arms out as if he were a soccer player who'd just scored a winning goal.

"You can all relax because I'm here now," he said.

"Last thing I'm going to do is relax," Oscar said. "Especially with you around."

They started hauling everything they would need out of the robotics closet: toolboxes, the two video monitors, and Stinky. They loaded up a cart and rolled the heavy stuff to the school van. Luis hefted the robot into the back and slammed the door.

Luis piled into the cramped cab of Fredi's truck with Oscar. Since they had graduated, they couldn't ride in a school vehicle, which was fine with Luis. The van was jammed with equipment, and he was happy not to have to listen to Lorenzo's comments on everything he saw out the window. The guy talked too much.

They were happily on their way when out of nowhere, Lorenzo's voice blasted inside Fredi's truck. "Wassup, wassup?"

Luis groaned at realizing that Dr. Cameron had given each car a two-way radio.

Lorenzo's voice crackled over the radio as they zipped along I-10, heading west. "We need to review our engineering presentation."

Luis knew that nearly half the points in the contest would come from how well they defended their ideas in front of the judges. Each of them had to be ready to answer any question. This was the part that scared Luis the most. The team had been using flashcards to study, and they would quiz each other sometimes, but Luis was still struggling.

"What's a PWM cable?" Dr. Cameron asked over the radio.

"PWM," Lorenzo said, "is pulse-width modulation. It controls analog circuits with digital output."

Then the moment Luis was dreading came. "Yo, Luis," Lorenzo said over the radio. "What's the index of refraction?"

Luis looked at Oscar. He could see the doubt on his friend's face.

"Do you know it?" Oscar asked.

"Uhhh . . ." Luis wasn't totally sure, but he thought he knew. He spoke into the radio and said, "It's about light and water. About how fast light goes through water."

"And what's the number?" Cristian radioed.

Luis didn't know. He looked out the window, and the silence hung in the air.

"Okay, Luis, here's what we are going to do," Oscar said, taking the radio. "We are going to drill you."

Soon, the Sonoran Desert airwaves filled with questions about spike relays, underwater camera housings, and transmitter frequencies. They went back and forth until they crossed the California border. Luis was worried. *This is hard*, he thought.

But then outside, in the fields around the town of Blythe, Luis saw farmworkers picking watermelons in the scorching 100-degree heat. *Now* that *is hard*, he reminded himself.

PART THREE

LORENZO

THE TEAM ROLLED INTO SANTA BARBARA IN THE AFTERNOON AND made their way onto the University of California campus. A gloomy layer of mist hung over the Pacific Ocean and drifted around the area, covering the school in a blanket of gray. The cloudy skies didn't bother Lorenzo. He caught glimpses here and there of the Pacific and was enthralled. He hadn't gone on the trip to SeaBotix back in November, so this was the first time he'd seen the ocean.

"It's incredifying," he said, meaning it was both incredible and terrifying.

It was summer break, so the campus was pretty empty, but South Hall was crowded with all the teams participating in the robotics competition.

Lorenzo helped the team unload the equipment into the dorm room they had been assigned. Together they spent the night making sure that everything still worked. They pushed one of the beds onto its side and planted Stinky on the floor. When they turned the power on, the propellers refused to reverse. Then, when they let go of the joysticks, the robot whirred into action. It seemed as if a ghost were operating it.

"Es brujería," Lorenzo said.

It was the last thing they needed the night before the competition. A bewitched robot that wouldn't even respond to their commands. But after an hour, the controls mysteriously started working again. It was as if the desert heat they'd driven through had tweaked Stinky's brain. Lorenzo was relieved that they didn't have to take the robot apart to figure out what was wrong. How would they have rebuilt it?

It had been a long day of travel, and this last scare made them feel a little tense, too. The ocean was within walking distance. Lorenzo wanted to explore the beautiful beaches, but they all went to sleep early.

AROUND NINE THE NEXT MORNING, LORENZO AND THE REST OF THE team rolled Stinky into a UCSB pool reserved for practice. The other teams scattered around the pool looked their way. When Lorenzo saw the other teams' robots, his eyes almost dropped from their sockets. The robots on display looked like works of art! He quickly made a list of all the things the other competitors had been able to get: glass syntactic foam, machined metal, elaborate control panels, and cool matching outfits. Lorenzo had thought that his paint job was nice. Now, as he stared at Stinky, the robot looked like a clown.

They shuffled to a corner of the pool that wasn't taken.

"Damn," Lorenzo muttered as he caught a glimpse of the MIT team. He saw a large EXXONMOBIL sticker and guessed the company had donated money to them. Their ROV was the smallest, most densely instrumented robot at the competition. The group wore matching blue shirts emblazoned with the words MIT ROV TEAM.

"I've never seen so many white people in one place," Lorenzo said. As he looked at the team members' pale skin and blond hair, he felt intimidated. They seemed to have power, a power Lorenzo, as a poor immigrant kid, had never had.

"Come on—let's focus," Oscar ordered. They were scheduled to appear for their engineering review that afternoon, which meant they had only a few hours to practice in the pool. Every second counted now.

Luis gently lowered Stinky into the water. "It's ready," he grunted. Oscar and Cristian motored Stinky forward and down, but the robot started turning.

"Go straight!" Fredi shouted.

"I *am* going straight," Oscar responded.

"No, you're not—you're going left," Fredi said.

"Let me try," Cristian said, taking the controls from Oscar. He tried to get the robot to bank right, but it wasn't working.

"Pull it out!" Cristian shouted to Luis.

Luis speedily pulled Stinky to the surface and lifted it out of the water. They gathered around the dripping robot. Lorenzo opened the briefcase top and looked inside.

"It's got to be the programming," Fredi said.

"It's not the programming," Dr. Cameron snapped.

"It's the water," Lorenzo said. Everybody looked at him. "The water got in." He pointed to the tablespoon of water on the bottom of the briefcase.

"Why didn't it just short out?" Cristian asked.

He gently pressed the PWM wires connecting the joysticks to

the control board. The robot's propellers whirred to life. At first, it seemed like good news. The robot was still working. Lorenzo ran his fingers through his long hair and shook his head.

"Guys, we've got two problems. The cables need to be re-soldered. And we got a leak."

OSCAR

BACK IN THEIR DORM ROOM, OSCAR WAS WORRIED. THE ROBOT wasn't working, and the team was scheduled to go in front of the judges in two hours. Stinky was turning out to be a failure from the start. Would they be beaten before the competition had even begun?

No, Oscar wasn't ready to give up. "Let's take it apart," he argued. "We can fix it."

"Look, don't worry about the robot right now," Fredi said. "We've got all night to troubleshoot."

"It's more important to get ready for the review," Dr. Cameron agreed.

Oscar couldn't hide his shaken confidence, and by looking at Cristian, Lorenzo, and Luis, he knew they had the same fears. Would they end up leaving Santa Barbara sure that the whole thing was a mistake? That they should have never dared to be ambitious?

"Everybody come with me," Dr. Cameron commanded. Fredi and the team followed him out of the dorm to a bridge. Though it was summertime, there was still a steady flow of pedestrians. "I want you guys to hang out here and talk to anybody who comes by," he said.

"What do you want us to talk about?" Oscar asked. What was Dr. Cameron up to? Oscar was in no mood to talk to strangers.

"Say, 'Hi, would you like to hear about our thrusters?'" Dr. Cameron prompted.

Lorenzo snickered. "I don't think nobody is going to talk to us if we say that."

Dr. Cameron persevered. "Tell them you built a robot. They'll want to hear about it."

"They're just going to think we are begging for money," Oscar said.

"Give it a try," Fredi said.

Fredi and Dr. Cameron walked off and watched from a distance.

Oscar saw some people heading their way, and he just wanted to run back to the room and hide. He and his friends were too shy and embarrassed, so they let those people walk by. Oscar gripped the plastic three-ring binder that contained drawings of Stinky's innovations. *Come on—don't be a coward*, he told himself. But he couldn't do it. He was the team's leader, but this time, it wasn't he who took the lead.

Lorenzo was the one who had the courage to talk to a man who looked like a professor. "Hi, we're high school students from Phoenix, and we're here to compete in the underwater-robotics contest. Do you want to hear about it?"

The man laughed. "Okay. What does your robot do?"

No longer afraid, Oscar stepped forward with his three-ring binder and flipped to the first page, which showed a photo of Stinky. "It's an ROV. That means 'remotely operated vehicle.'" He explained that Stinky was designed to retrieve underwater objects, record video, sample fluid, measure distances, and locate sounds.

"It can do all that?" the man said.

"When it's working, yeah," Oscar said. "Right now, it's kind of messed up."

"Well, I'll be rooting for you," the man said, and, after wishing them luck, headed away.

After that, the team stopped all kinds of people and explained why their robot was so cool, even if it was on life support. Cristian talked about applying the index of refraction to their laser range findings, and Lorenzo bragged about his "ghetto" liquid sampling tool. The people they talked to seemed impressed, and the reactions they got gave Oscar and the others a boost of confidence. It reminded them that they were doing something they had never done before. In Phoenix, they were called "illegal aliens" and lived in fear of being arrested and deported. Oscar was tired of fighting to make people see him as a true American. No, at this moment, he didn't care about proving how American he was. Right now, he just wanted to be a normal teenager at an underwater-robotics competition by the ocean.

CRISTIAN

IN THE HALLWAY OUTSIDE THE REVIEW ROOM, CRISTIAN AND HIS teammates waited nervously to be called in. He knew that the panel was made up of some impressive judges, and he was scared. He was just a skinny, five-foot-two science nerd at a school where 71.17 percent of students got free or subsidized lunches because they were below the poverty line. He was a kid who lived in an eight-foot-by-eight-foot plywood box slapped onto the side of a trailer in a mobile-home park. What was he doing here?

Maybe coming to the competition was a mistake.

He thought of all the white college students his team was competing against. They had arrived at the competition with extraordinary underwater machines. They were made of machined metal, and some teams had budgets of thousands of dollars. And what had Cristian and his team shown up with? A multicolored plastic robot that was partially put together from spare parts and glued together with stinky blue glue.

They were going to be embarrassed in front of everyone.

"Are you guys coming with us?" Cristian asked Fredi and Dr. Cameron. Teachers were allowed to be in the room with their teams, and more than ever, he needed his teachers beside him.

Dr. Cameron and Fredi looked at each other. "No, you guys go solo. You got this," Fredi said.

"But—!" Cristian almost panicked. The teachers had always been there, always.

"Carl Hayden Community High School?" a woman with a clipboard called as she came out of the review room.

Reluctantly, Cristian and the other boys went in. Backed by a green chalkboard, they stood nervously at the front of the classroom, a swarm of desks crowded in the space between them and the three judges.

Cristian felt sweat gathering on his forehead.

"How'd you make the laser range finder work?" Tom Swean asked. He ran the navy's Ocean Engineering and Marine Systems program.

"We used a helium-neon laser," Cristian answered quickly, feeling his adrenaline shoot up. "We captured its phase shift with a CCD camera and manually corrected by thirty percent to account for the index of refraction."

He saw Mr. Swean raise a bushy, graying eyebrow. *Did I say something wrong?* Cristian wondered.

Lisa Spence, the flight lead at NASA's Neutral Buoyancy Laboratory, sat next to Mr. Swean. "There aren't oceans in Phoenix," she pointed out.

"No, ma'am," Lorenzo said. "But we got pools."

Mr. Swean followed up with a question on signal interference. Cristian looked at Oscar.

"Sir, we experimented with a fifteen-meter cable and found very low levels of interference," Oscar answered. "So, we decided to extend our tether to thirty-three meters."

"You're very comfortable with the metric system," Mr. Swean observed.

"I grew up in Mexico, sir," Oscar said proudly. "In Mexico, people don't measure in feet but in meters."

Mr. Swean nodded. He looked through their simple flip chart. "Why don't you have a PowerPoint display?"

"PowerPoint is a distraction," Cristian said. "People use it when they don't know what to say."

"And you know what to say?"

"Yes, sir."

So far, Cristian, Lorenzo, and Oscar had been able to speak intelligently about their robot's mechanical and electronic parts. But it was meant to be a team effort, and the judges needed to see if *all* team members could answer questions. The moment that Cristian was dreading finally came. One of the judges looked at Luis. He hadn't said anything yet.

"You used PWM cables," she said to Luis. "Can you tell me what role they play?"

Cristian held his breath as all eyes turned to his six-foot, 220-pound teammate. Luis rarely said much of anything, so it was hard to tell what he was thinking. Cristian wanted to answer for him but held back.

"PWM means 'pulse-width modulation,'" Luis answered, looking completely calm. "It's a technique for converting an analog signal to digital. A lot of our sensors are analog, but our microprocessor is digital, so we used PWM cables to connect them."

Cristian couldn't believe it: It was spot-on! He wanted to hug Luis.

Most of the teams had been in the review room for forty-five minutes, but Team Stinky was done in twenty-five.

"How'd you do, guys?" Dr. Cameron said as Cristian walked out, followed by the rest of the team. Fredi and Dr. Cameron saw them trying to hide their disappointment.

Cristian looked at Oscar, Lorenzo, and Luis. Their faces showed no emotion. Then suddenly, they burst out laughing.

"We did great!" they shouted.

The trial they had been dreading was over. Now came the fun part. But the strain was intense. The team had to repair their robot before its scheduled competition in the morning. They had less than twenty-four hours to fix both the leak and the loose wiring.

"We have to get to work," Cristian said.

"Not yet," Dr. Cameron said.

"That's right. We're going to Sizzler," Fredi said. "Nobody will solve anything without a full belly."

LORENZO

ON THE SHORT VAN RIDE TO THE RESTAURANT, THE TEAM TOSSED around ideas about how to take care of the leak. "There's no way we can buy a new briefcase and get everything rewired in time. We need to come up with something quick and easy," Oscar said.

"You need a desiccant," Fredi said. "Something that will soak up the moisture."

"But it's got to fit inside the case," Cristian pointed out. "It's got to be small and superabsorbent."

A popular television ad flashed through Lorenzo's mind. "Absorbent? Like a tampon?"

Oscar, Cristian, and Luis laughed. It sounded ridiculous to them.

"Actually, that's a perfect idea," Fredi said.

AFTER ORDERING THE ALL-YOU-CAN-EAT DINNER AND DOWNING more shrimp than he'd consumed in his life, Lorenzo found himself standing in the parking lot of a Ralphs grocery store near the UCSB campus. Behind him, in the van, his teammates egged him on.

"Go on," Oscar said. "It was your idea."

"So why do I have to get them? Somebody else should have to."

"Go," Oscar ordered.

"I don't know which ones to get."

"So ask someone."

Lorenzo headed for the store. It was done up to look like a hacienda, complete with a red-tile roof, glaringly white walls, and freshly planted palms. He walked inside and wandered past the organic-produce section, trying to build up his courage. He passed an elderly lady examining vegetables. He was too embarrassed to ask her. Next, he saw a young blond woman in designer jeans shopping for shampoo.

"Excuse me, miss." He wasn't used to going up to women by himself, let alone well-dressed white women. He saw the worry flash across her face. Maybe she thought he was trying to sell magazines or candy bars or worse—begging for money. But he steeled himself.

He explained that he was building a robot for an underwater contest sponsored by NASA, and his robot was leaking. He wanted to soak up the water with tampons but didn't know which ones to buy. "Could you help me buy the most best tampons?"

The woman broke into a big smile and sighed with relief. "Yes, follow me."

She led him to the feminine-hygiene section and handed him a box of o.b. Ultra. "These are the most absorbent and don't have an applicator, so they'll be easier to fit inside your robot."

He stared at the ground, feeling his cheeks burning.

"Ummm . . . thanks, miss."

As he headed quickly for the checkout, the young woman called out to him, "I hope you win!"

OSCAR

THEY GOT BACK TO THEIR DORM ROOM AND CIRCLED UP AROUND Stinky. A bunch of the joystick wires had come off from the controller, and there was no way they could just resolder the few that had popped loose. They had to pull all the wires and start over. All *sixty-four* wires. It would take hours, and they were already tired from the tension of the engineering review and the morning's failed practice session. Plus, they were stuffed with steak and shrimp and breadsticks.

Everybody just wanted to go to sleep, but they had only until dawn to get the robot working.

"I'll stay up and do it," Oscar volunteered.

"I'll do it with you," Lorenzo offered.

Over the past nine months, Oscar hadn't taken Lorenzo seriously. The long-haired guy cracked jokes and had weird ideas— okay, most of them *did* work—but throughout the year, Oscar had been preparing himself for Lorenzo to flake out, drop off the team, and never show up again.

But in this moment, Oscar realized that Lorenzo was very committed. Good engineering solutions had value. But, to Oscar, doing things that no one else wanted to do, toughing it out and soldiering through, that's what counted. For the first time, he felt real respect for his teammate.

"All right, let's do it," Oscar said. "You and me."

Luis and Cristian went to sleep in another room. Dr. Cameron took a bed in the corner, and Fredi had to sleep on the floor with just a pillow and a blanket and all the lights on. Stinky sat where the other bed used to be—they had flipped it up and propped it against the wall.

Oscar and Lorenzo hunched over the electronics on the carpet. Sixty-four wires, each little bigger than a single hair, needed to be carefully refitted into individual small holes in the circuit board and then secured with a touch of solder.

Lorenzo placed the wires in the holes, while Oscar melted the solder with the soldering iron. With each drop of solder, a small puff of gray smoke curled into the air. They barely talked during the delicate, nerve-racking work. If Oscar hit the bare wire with the soldering iron, the wire was so thin that it would instantly melt and disappear, forcing them to pull out everything they'd done, cut back and re-strip all the wires, and start over.

By the time they had done fifty wires, it was roughly two in the morning. Their eyes hurt after hours of staring at tiny wires. The stakes were higher, too. A mistake now would mean ripping out more than four dozen completed connections. If that happened, they wouldn't have enough time to resolder everything before the competition. Each connection needed to be perfect now.

"Let's take a break for a second," Oscar said.

They sat back and rubbed their eyes. The room was filled with an acrid, burnt smell from all their soldering work. Everybody else was asleep.

"Thanks for staying up with me," Oscar said.

"You think I'm going to let you do this by yourself?" Lorenzo said.

Oscar thought he meant that they were all in this together until Lorenzo added, "You'd probably screw it up if I wasn't watching you."

Lorenzo grinned at him with a big, goofy, crooked-tooth smile. Oscar chuckled. He never would have been friends with a kid like Lorenzo, but now he was glad they were teammates.

"Shut up," Oscar said, picking up the soldering gun. "Let's get this done."

They had fourteen left. Oscar moved slowly and carefully while Lorenzo positioned the fifty-first wire.

Lorenzo said a silent prayer to the Virgen de Guadalupe, and they worked through the final batch of wires, connecting the last one around two thirty A.M. They turned the power on and tested the joysticks. The robot worked!

The boys were exhausted but excited as they hit the sack. As he tried to quiet down his racing thoughts, Oscar couldn't shake one worry: Would it still work when the sun came up?

LUIS

THE NEXT MORNING, LUIS READ THE BANNER ABOVE THE LARGE outdoor pool: WELCOME TO THE 2004 NATIONAL ROV COMPETITION. A set of high-powered fans blew across the surface of the fifteen-foot-deep pool so that no one could see underwater from the surface. Luis could make out the blurry outline of a large black structure but nothing more. A loudspeaker blared Hawaiian music. This was the main event. The underwater portion of the Explorer-class competition had begun.

Monterey Peninsula College was called to the pool. Luis was shocked at how big their team was—fifteen crew members! And they had *three* vehicles: two ROVs and a third craft, which served as their eyes in the sky. It floated on the surface of the water with a camera system to guide the underwater operation.

But even with all that robotic firepower, Monterey picked up only 30 out of 110 points.

Luis was worried. *If that college couldn't do it, how can the Carl Hayden team do it?* The mission tasks were proving to be even more difficult than he'd anticipated.

He had memorized the list of main tasks:

- **Measure the submarine's length**
- **Calculate its depth**
- **Navigate inside the submarine to recover the captain's bell**
- **Recover a lost piece of research equipment**
- **Recover a sonar device that would be lying on the pool bottom**
- **Sample liquid out of the secret-cargo barrels**
- **Take the temperature of water seeping out of a cold-water spring**

Cape Fear Community College from North Carolina did a little better. Their robot had a beautiful aluminum frame covered with a shiny blue fiberglass foam. They called it the Sea Devil 3. It gleamed so nicely in the morning sun that, to Luis, it looked like an underwater piece of jewelry. But despite their beautiful robot and its fancy movements, the college managed to post only 40 points by the end of their thirty-minute run.

There were eleven teams in the Explorer division. Luis was relieved to see that for some of the teams, their missions were complete disasters. Their robots sank to the bottom of the pool and sat there without moving. After a few minutes of trying to fix the problem, the teams had no choice but to haul their robots out of the water and quit. One stranded robot let out a giant air bubble as it was being pulled up.

Sitting next to him, Lorenzo laughed. "It farted!"

Luis laughed, too, but he soon got worried again. If these other teams were struggling, it meant that his team would have an even tougher time. What were they thinking choosing the Explorer division? It was clearly punishingly difficult. Maybe they should have competed with the high schools instead of the colleges. Too late now.

But then Luis became hopeful. If they could just get their robot to work and complete at least one of the seven tasks, they'd be ahead of the teams whose robots had shorted out. That meant they wouldn't finish last.

The judges called MIT to the pool, and the college from Boston lowered their compact welded-aluminum ROV into the water. Luis held his breath as he watched their ten-thousand-dollar robot pile up points.

MIT wasn't perfect, though. They found the barrel with the leaking fluid and moved up to it. This task was worth 15 points—more than any other. But they couldn't get their sampling tube into the barrel. The opening was too narrow. They gave up and sped away.

Oscar shook his head. "I told you the task was impossible."

When MIT finished, they had 48 points, putting them in first place.

IT WAS ALMOST TEAM STINKY'S TURN. ON THE EDGE OF THE POOL, Luis watched as Lorenzo crammed tampons around Stinky's circuit board in the briefcase, lining the edges with clumps of the cottony things.

"Put one over there," Oscar ordered, pointing to a corner of the briefcase.

"I know what I'm doing," Lorenzo said, ignoring Oscar. "I think I earned the right to put them wherever I want!"

"We need Carl Hayden Community High School on deck," one of the judges said over the PA system.

Their time had come.

"Okay, guys," Dr. Cameron told them. "You probably won't have more than ten minutes before the leak shorts the controls, so go as fast as you can for the easy stuff."

"Just get some points," Fredi said. "That'll put you ahead of a lot of teams."

"We will," Oscar said confidently.

Luis flexed his muscles and set out to do what he was here for. He helped roll the equipment toward the "command shack," a kind of tent enclosed on three sides.

The judges started a timer. Like the other contestants, Carl Hayden had five minutes to set up inside the shack and complete a safety check.

"Let's do this!" Oscar said.

Everybody burst into action. Oscar and Lorenzo rolled their monitor cart into position inside the tent. Cristian carried a piece of particleboard that held the joysticks and topside electronics. Luis off-loaded Stinky onto the edge of the pool and handed the tether to Cristian, who connected it to the control system. Lorenzo fitted a purple balloon onto Stinky's bilge pump. Oscar flipped on the power switch.

Stinky was operational.

"You guys are clear to get wet," a judge said. "You've got thirty minutes."

"Okay, Luis, let's go," Oscar said.

Luis hefted their machine off the deck and lowered Stinky into the water.

"Virgen de Guadalupe, please protect us!" Lorenzo prayed. "Please let the tampons work."

The propellers whirred. Luis stood at the pool's edge, paying out the tether cable. He watched Stinky move wildly as it dived toward the bottom.

CRISTIAN

FROM INSIDE THE CONTROL SHACK, CRISTIAN, OSCAR, AND LORENZO watched Stinky's descent on their video screens. From the robot's front-facing camera, they could see the bright, sparkling water that Stinky was moving through.

"There's something there." Cristian pointed. Down below, they could see a black object on an elevated tarp. It was the towfish, a mock-up of an underwater sonar device designed to be trailed behind a vessel. Just seeing it was worth 5 points. The judges standing behind them in the command shack made a notation. With 5 points, they were tied for last place.

"Vamos, Cristian, this is it!" Oscar said, pushing his controls too far forward. They were nervous and overcompensated for each other's joystick movements, causing Stinky to go off course. The towfish and tarp disappeared off their screens.

"Go back!" Cristian said.

"I got it." Oscar corrected course, and they sped down toward the object.

"You're going too fast," Cristian said.

Oscar hit REVERSE, and the propeller blast pushed the towfish off the tarp. They circled the tarp but could no longer reach the towfish.

"Let's do the next thing," Oscar said hurriedly. He didn't want to waste any time.

"What's that?" Lorenzo asked, pointing to an object on the screen. It looked like a barrel.

"It's the fluid-sampling thing," Cristian said.

"That's last," Oscar said. "Let's keep moving."

They rotated and saw the big black submarine in the distance. So far, Stinky was holding up well. The joysticks were working, and the robot responded to all their commands. Oscar pushed forward, and Stinky motored toward the submarine. Cristian pulled back, and Stinky moved toward the surface.

"Let's try to do the measuring," Oscar said.

They managed to hook the loop of their tape measure onto the end of the submarine and reversed, spooling out the tape. When they reached the end of the sub, Lorenzo flicked on the black-and-white camera that was pointed at the tape measure. The screen was pure white.

"I can't see anything," Oscar said.

The camera exposure had been set when they were indoors at Scuba Sciences. During their practice run the previous day, it had been cloudy in Santa Barbara. Now the sun was shining strongly, and the light overwhelmed the iris of the camera. The measurement was there—they just couldn't see it.

Still, they got 5 points for using the tape measure. They motored over to the sub's "periscope"—a tall plastic tube—and aimed their laser range finder at the bottom to take the depth. Again, it gave a reading, but the image coming from the camera was blown out in the bright sunlight, and they couldn't see it. They got 5 points for being able to hover beside the periscope while taking the depth, even if they couldn't actually report the measurement.

Most of the remaining tasks needed them to go inside the submarine, a dangerous effort.

"I hope Stinky doesn't get snagged," Oscar said.

Cristian was worried, too. If the robot's tether got caught on something, it would be game over.

Oscar checked the time: They had fifteen minutes left. "Let's go back to the barrel."

"I thought we were going to do that last," Cristian said.

"Let's just try it." Oscar spun the robot and headed back toward the barrel.

Cristian remembered that when they'd practiced in the pool in Phoenix, they usually couldn't place Stinky's bent copper proboscis into a half-inch pipe. The few times they did, it took dozens of tries. Now the minutes were counting down on their mission. Cristian wasn't sure it was worth trying, but Oscar was in charge.

They wiped the sweat from their palms and gripped the joysticks again. They looked carefully at the monitors as Stinky approached the barrel that had frustrated the MIT team. The "barrel" was a one-gallon paint can. A half-inch tube stuck out of it.

Everyone in the control shack was silent. Now that they were focused on the mission, both Oscar and Cristian relaxed and made tiny movements with their joysticks. Oscar tapped his control forward while Cristian gave a short backward blast on the vertical propellers. As Stinky floated forward a half inch, its rear raised up, and the sampling pipe sank perfectly into the drum.

"Dios mio," Oscar whispered, not fully believing what he saw.

"Hit the switches!" Cristian nearly shrieked.

Lorenzo had already activated the pump and was counting out twenty seconds in a decidedly unscientific way.

"Uno, dos, tres, cuatro . . . ," he mumbled until he got to twenty. He turned off the pump. They couldn't see if the balloon inside its milk-jug basket had filled, so there was no telling if it had worked.

"Let's get it to Luis," Oscar said.

Oscar backed Stinky out of the barrel. They spun the robot around and piloted it back to Luis at the edge of the pool. Cristian watched Luis haul Stinky out of the water. He and the others ran out of the command shack. The purple balloon sat inside Lorenzo's hacked-open milk container. Cristian could see there was something inside! He just hoped it wasn't the pool water.

Oscar carefully removed the balloon. Cristian grabbed a plastic graduated cylinder to measure the fluid inside. Finding the barrel was worth 5 points. Collecting a sample and returning it to the control shack was worth another 5. They'd get 1 additional point for every hundred milliliters they collected—up to five hundred milliliters—for a total of 5 possible extra points. Oscar began to pour the liquid into the cylinder.

"Cien, doscientos, trescientos," Cristian said with mounting excitement as Oscar poured in the fluid. Finally, quinientos—five hundred milliliters. They had collected a complete, though slightly diluted, sample and would receive a whopping 12 points!

That brought them to 27 points so far, more than most of the other teams.

"Can we make a little noise?" Cristian asked Pat Barrow, a NASA lab operations manager supervising the contest.

"Go on ahead," he replied.

Cristian started yelling.

Lorenzo hooted and slapped everyone on the back. "That was *frictastic!*"

"What does that even mean?" Cristian said.

Lorenzo smiled. "It means frickin' fantastic."

Cristian stood there with a silly grin on his face while his friends danced around him. They had done something that some of the best engineering students in the country had failed to accomplish.

"Let's go, let's go!" Oscar said, cutting the celebration short. "We're not done yet!"

They still had ten minutes left, and they couldn't waste any more time. They now had a shot at a top spot in the competition. Luis quickly lowered the ROV back into the water.

Oscar piloted Stinky toward the submarine. They hadn't explored the interior, and there were a lot more points to be won. Cristian kept Stinky leveled as Oscar drove it forward. The robot inched into the structure, trailing its tether. The walls were black, and the passageway was too narrow. The tether began to grind against the structure, pulling them back. Seconds ticked away and they weren't getting anywhere.

"We've got to do something different," Oscar said.

With a minute left, Oscar tried to make a tight turn, and the prop wash blew open a compartment, revealing a golden bell.

"That's the captain's bell!" Cristian shouted.

As the time ran out on their mission, the judges marked them down for another 5 points for spotting the bell. That meant they had a total of 32 points. Not only had they not finished last, their mission score put them in third place behind MIT and Cape Fear Community College. Everything would be determined now by the scores they'd received from their earlier interview with the judges.

Fredi and Dr. Cameron rushed to the command shack. Fredi snapped picture after picture of the team, and Cristian felt like a celebrity.

OSCAR

THE AWARDS CEREMONY TOOK PLACE OVER DINNER, AND OSCAR was glad for that. He felt as if he had run twenty miles with a fifty-pound rucksack. He was so hungry that even the flavorless iceberg-lettuce salad looked good to him. He felt his nerves calming down.

"You kids did great," Fredi said. "I'm sure you probably placed somewhere in the middle."

Oscar sighed. He knew Fredi was trying to get them to lower their expectations, but he couldn't help getting his hopes up. But didn't he know better than that? He remembered his failed army dream and returned to reality.

"We'll just be proud of what we've accomplished, right, guys?"

Cristian, Lorenzo, and Luis nodded.

The first award was a surprise—a special prize that wasn't listed in the program.

"The judges have created this prize spontaneously to honor special achievement," the awards announcer said. He stood behind a podium on the temporary stage and glanced down at his notes. The contestants sat crowded around a dozen tables, waiting to hear which team would be receiving the prize.

"Carl Hayden Community High School," the announcer said, "please come up."

"Whoa!" Lorenzo said.

Oscar felt a wave of disappointment as he led the team up to the stage, forcing a smile. It seemed obvious that this was just a pat on the back, a pity prize. As if the judges felt sorry for the Mexican kids from a poor school. He felt as if the judges were saying, *You did well, considering where you came from.*

As he listened to the clapping around him, Oscar knew he didn't want to be "special"—he wanted third. Did getting this prize mean they hadn't placed anywhere near the top?

They returned to their seats, and Fredi and Dr. Cameron shook their hands.

"Good job, guys," Fredi said. "You did well." Seeing Oscar's disappointment, Fredi said, "Hey, you got an award. Everybody back home is going to be really proud of you."

Oscar nodded. Fredi was right. The whole team had come

further than even they had expected. Maybe they hadn't placed at the top of the rankings, but everybody now knew that they were talented engineers. That was a pretty remarkable accomplishment on its own. He felt as if he were part of a group of superheroes.

At seeing his friends' gloomy faces, Oscar reacted as he usually did. "Come on, guys," he said encouragingly. "This is great. For the rest of our lives, we can say we won an award here."

The guys looked down at the award certificates they were holding.

"I guess they look pretty cool," Cristian said.

Lorenzo was the only one who was beaming. "No one has ever clapped for me before," he said. "I'll remember it forever."

LORENZO

THE CEREMONY WAS COMING TO AN END. A FEW SMALL PRIZES WERE handed out and then finally, it was time for the bigger awards: Design Elegance, Technical Report, and Overall Winner.

Lorenzo saw the MIT students shift around in their seats and stretch their legs. Their robot couldn't do the fluid sampling, but they had completed more underwater tasks overall than any other team.

He looked at the Cape Fear College team. They sat across the room, fidgeted with their napkins, and tried not to appear nervous. They had posted the second-highest number of points during the underwater mission.

Lorenzo then scanned the room, and his eyes fell on the students from Monterey Peninsula College. They'd placed fourth behind Carl Hayden in the underwater trials. *They probably got third*, Lorenzo thought. He knew it all came down to how the judges graded the teams' oral and written presentations.

Lorenzo glanced back at the buffet table and wondered if he could get more cake before the ceremony wrapped up.

Then the announcer leaned into the microphone and said, "And the winner of the Design Award is . . . the ROV named Stinky!"

"What did he just say?" Lorenzo asked, looking away from the cake.

"Oh my God!" Fredi shouted. "Stand up!"

It didn't make any sense to Lorenzo. There was nothing pretty or elegant about their robot. Compared to the gleaming machines other teams had built, Stinky was a simple multicolored clown. The PVC, the balloon, the tape measure—in each case they had chosen the most straightforward solution to a problem. It was what Lorenzo had learned from watching his godfather fix cars. It was what Oscar had learned in JROTC. It was what Cristian had learned gathering junk that had fallen out of the sky in the desert. It was what Luis had learned working in the kitchen.

Lorenzo would later find out that this was exactly what had impressed the judges. They believed there was no reason to come up with a difficult solution when a simple one was enough. Stinky had more things in common with the machines at NASA than Lorenzo realized.

He could see that he wasn't the only one in shock. His teammates looked at one another and sat as if glued to their seats.

"Come on, guys, move it!" Oscar said.

They marched back up to the stage and looked out at the audience clapping for them. Lorenzo felt a rush of emotion. The judges' special prize wasn't a pity award. These people were giving them real recognition.

"Thank you, sir," Lorenzo said as he and the team started to walk off the stage.

"Stay where you are," the announcer said. He turned to the audience and said, "Carl Hayden Community High School is also the winner of the Technical Writing Award."

Lorenzo didn't know what was happening. It seemed impossible that they would win three awards, and for writing? *Us illiterate people from the desert?* Lorenzo thought. He looked at Cristian, who had been responsible for a large part of the writing.

"We're just a bunch of ESL students," Cristian said softly.

How could four English language learners have produced a better written report than kids from one of the country's top engineering schools?

After the additional award certificates were handed out, the team went back to their table, and the applause sounded even louder. To Lorenzo it felt like a dream.

WHEN THE ROOM QUIETED DOWN, THE AUDIENCE WAS READY FOR THE announcement of the top three winners of the overall competition. They were now a highly decorated underwater-robotics team. It had been an amazing run, something Lorenzo and his friends would remember forever.

The announcer began the countdown. "Third place goes to Cape Fear Community College," he said. There was a round of applause. Sea Devil 3, their ROV, was a work of art with powerful abilities and got the second-highest number of mission points.

"I thought they would get second," Cristian said.

Lorenzo knew that MIT would win the championship, so he figured that Monterey Peninsula College had managed to grab second place. They were a solid team who had performed well underwater and likely aced the engineering review.

"Maybe we got fourth place," Luis said shyly.

"Yeah, that'd be cool," Lorenzo said.

After the applause for Cape Fear died down, the announcer cleared his throat for the next announcement. "And second place goes to MIT," he said into the microphone.

There was a feeling of shock in the room.

Cristian looked at Fredi.

"MIT got second?" Cristian blurted.

"So who won first place?" Lorenzo asked.

"And the winner of the Marine Advanced Technology Education ROV Explorer-class championship goes to . . ."

The announcer started drumming on the podium. A deep rumble rose up around the room as others joined in.

Only nine months earlier, Lorenzo and his teammates hadn't known what an ROV was. They were poor Mexican immigrants who had grown up undocumented in the United States and attended a so-called ghetto school. There was no way they could win.

The announcer stopped drumming. The room fell silent, and he leaned into the microphone.

"Carl Hayden Community High School!" he shouted.

The 2004 MATE Robotics Competition was not going to a big-league university or a team of seasoned competitors. It was going to four high school students who had simply hoped not to finish last.

To his shock, Lorenzo saw the students from MIT stand up and begin to clap. Other competitors stood as well, and by the time he and the team made it to the stage, most of the room was on its feet. They were getting a standing ovation. The audience roared their support.

The kids from the desert had won.

"WE BEAT MIT!" CRISTIAN SCREAMED OUT TO THE OCEAN.

They had hiked a mile down the dark beach. They couldn't contain themselves inside the awards hall and had gotten out as quickly as they could. They didn't want to be rude, but it was too much to handle without a little yelling.

"We woooooon!" Oscar hollered into the night sky, the full moon shining down on them.

"*AHHHRHGHG!*" Luis roared. He was so loud, everyone fell silent.

The night was quiet—just the sound of the waves crashing softly. Lorenzo couldn't take his eyes off the ocean. It felt like a living thing to him. He had never imagined its immensity. From seeing it on television, he would have never known how magnificent it was.

"I want you guys to know how proud I am of you," Dr. Cameron said.

"From now on, you guys are the team that beat MIT," Fredi told them. "You know what that makes you?"

"What?" Cristian asked.

"Badasses," Fredi said, smiling.

"Damn," Lorenzo said. "I'm a badass."

Fredi took a picture of them standing by the shore that night. They threw their fists in the air. Oscar held up his index finger to signal that they were number one. Standing on the beach with his friends and the teachers who believed in them, the ocean breeze playing with his long hair and lovingly caressing his pear-shaped head, Lorenzo knew this was a day he would never forget.

AFTERWORD BY THE AUTHOR

THIS STORY

ON NOVEMBER 1, 2004, I RECEIVED A STRANGE EMAIL ABOUT A HIGH
school robotics team in Phoenix, Arizona. The email was about
Cristian, Oscar, Luis, and Lorenzo and the robot, Stinky. I write
for *Wired*, a technology magazine, and so I get a lot of emails
from companies that want me to write about their products. I
had never gotten one from a high school.

I called the school to find out more. I ended up on the phone
with their coach Fredi Lajvardi, who was excited to talk. Over
the summer, a local TV station had aired a segment about Carl
Hayden Community High School's robotics success, but nobody
seemed to pay attention after that. I was the first national jour-
nalist to call.

"When there's a fight or something, the press is all over us," he
said. "We do something good, nobody pays attention."

The last time they had a brawl at the school, he told me, his
students piloted a small, homemade robot past the news crew
that had arrived. When that got little response, they drove circles
around the camera. That prompted a few questions, but the crew
largely ignored them. The journalists were there to talk about
thugs, not robots.

I was intrigued. "So just back up a bit. How did your kids end
up in an underwater-robotics competition?"

Fredi chuckled. "You're skeptical, right? So were the judges."

I decided to fly to Phoenix to learn more about the team and was disappointed when I saw Stinky. The robot did not look sophisticated. It wasn't until I heard the boys explain Stinky's capabilities that I understood they had accomplished something remarkable. It was all the more impressive given that they built the machine with very simple and low-cost parts.

I decided to write an article about their accomplishment for *Wired*. It attracted a lot of attention. The boys' success inspired a 2014 documentary called *Underwater Dreams* that was screened at the White House to launch National Robotics Week. Later that year, Farrar, Straus and Giroux published my book based on the article. It became a *New York Times* bestseller, and Reyna Grande adapted it into the young adult book you're reading now.

A feature-length movie based on the boys' story was released in 2015, but the movie ends when the boys win the competition in Santa Barbara. Of course, real life kept going and life doesn't always have a Hollywood ending.

CRISTIAN

CRISTIAN DREAMED OF GOING TO COLLEGE, BUT HIS HOPES FLAGGED when the air-conditioning unit in his family's trailer broke. Without AC, the trailer turned into an unlivable aluminum oven in the desert heat. His parents had to spend $3,000 of savings to buy a new unit—money that Cristian had hoped could be used to at least start college.

Still, he could throw himself into the robotics team. After winning the competition in Santa Barbara, he was a junior and had two more years of high school to compete. There were doubters out there, too. Some wondered if Santa Barbara had just been a fluke, a one-time freak occurrence. Cristian and Lorenzo—who also hadn't yet graduated—proved them wrong. They went on to the national championships both years and were strong competitors, consistently performing at or near the top of every division they entered.

Fredi urged Cristian to apply to MIT; it seemed like a natural fit. But to Cristian and his family, Boston seemed too far away, too foreign. His parents wanted to keep him close, given his immigration status. They felt better having him nearby.

Fredi switched gears and suggested Arizona State University, and Cristian agreed to apply during his senior year. He was enthusiastically accepted and became the first person in his family to go to college.

Unfortunately, the American Dream can be hard to come by. After a year of college, voters in Arizona passed a law that raised tuition for undocumented immigrants like Cristian. Even though he had spent most of his life in Arizona, voters didn't view him as an Arizona citizen and wanted him to pay more money to go to school there.

As a result, Cristian couldn't afford to keep going to school. He had scholarship money, but it wasn't enough to cover the higher tuition. So he dropped out.

Instead of going to school, he found work at Home Depot and was assigned to the floor-and-wall department, where he helped customers order carpets and blinds. When someone bought a particularly large order of tile, he would walk in front of the forklift waving a flag to clear a path down the aisles.

At home, he set up a small laboratory in the corner of his room. He bought a soldering iron for thirty dollars and kept his eye out for deals at Home Depot. When two hundred feet of doorbell wire went on sale for three dollars, he bought himself a spool and brought it home. Most nights, he stayed up late, inventing new machines from scavenged parts. He found a broken electric guitar on the street, repaired it, and made a sound-effects pedal for it. He designed a new wheel that could rotate in any direction. He kept a gallon of muriatic acid beside his bed to etch circuit boards. At night, amid the smell of solder and machine oil, he felt the most happy.

Eventually, the metal-working shop that his dad worked at had an opening and he applied. They accepted him and he began working alongside his father. That is where he works now.

LUIS

AFTER GRADUATION, LUIS STARTED WORKING TWO JOBS. DURING the day, he filed papers at a Social Security office. In the evenings, he still worked as a short-order cook. It seemed unrealistic to expect that his life would change that much. He assumed that Santa Barbara had been nothing more than a blip, a brief glimpse into the opportunities that other people had. He tried not to think too much about it.

But when people began to hear about the success of the Carl Hayden team, random supporters started sending checks to the school district to support the boys' education. It started as a trickle but built into a flood as the world found out about their achievements. All told, about $120,000 came into the scholarship fund.

Luis decided to pursue his love of cooking and used the scholarship money to enroll in Le Cordon Bleu College of Culinary Arts in nearby Scottsdale. It was like entering another world, the world he remembered seeing on TV when Julia Child cooked. He learned how to cook food from all over the world, from France to China. He spent a lot of time cooking with Lorenzo. They bickered over who made better salsa, but it was fun.

When COVID struck, Luis got very sick. He was in the hospital for a long time. He survived and is now living at home with his family, recovering.

LORENZO

IN MAY 2006, LORENZO WALKED UP TO THE STAGE IN THE AUDITORIUM
at Carl Hayden to receive his diploma. He was the first member
of his family to graduate from high school. It should have been
a happy day. At one time, the principal was on the verge of
expelling him. Now he was a nationally recognized robotics
star. But as Lorenzo shook hands with the principal onstage and
accepted the diploma, he scanned the crowd. His father hadn't
shown up.

Lorenzo tamped down his feelings and tried to focus on his
future. With his share of the scholarship money, he enrolled full-
time in Phoenix College's culinary studies program. When he
graduated, he called Luis and proposed a bold idea: They could
start their own restaurant together.

Luis liked the idea, and the two friends decided to start a
catering company. They named the business Neither Here Nor
There, a nod to their immigration status, and started with their
mothers' recipes. Their dishes evolved from there. They turned
their moms' traditional green mole sauce into a mole pesto by
adding basil, pine nuts, and cream. They catered weddings, church
retreats, baby showers, and quinceañeras. It was fun, but it wasn't
a steady job, so Lorenzo also worked as a dishwasher at St. Francis,
an upscale restaurant in central Phoenix.

His dishwashing abilities impressed his superiors, who promoted him to prep cook and then line cook.

After years of working multiple cooking jobs, Lorenzo and

Luis's catering business grew. Now Lorenzo owns a food truck and runs the business full-time. While he serves happy customers tacos, he tells them about the joy of building robots.

OSCAR

WHEN RANDOM STRANGERS BEGAN SENDING MONEY TO HELP HIM, everything changed for Oscar. He left his job as a construction worker and used the scholarship money to enroll full-time at Arizona State University starting in the fall of 2005. He decided to major in mechanical engineering and graduated in four years.

At his graduation, President Obama gave the commencement speech. The stadium was jammed with more than seventy thousand people. It was the largest graduation ceremony in American history. To Oscar's family's surprise, the president began talking about Oscar and awarded him "special honors" as an outstanding member of the class of 2009. There were about nine thousand graduates that year. Oscar was only one of three to receive the award from the president.

But nothing could change the fact that Oscar was not a legal resident of the United States. Even though he had a valuable college degree, businesses were barred from hiring him. The only way to fix the situation was to go back to Mexico and ask for permission to live in the United States.

So, soon after graduating, Oscar deported himself. He walked back into Mexico for the first time in ten years. The following day he lined up with hundreds of others at the US consulate to apply for legal residency in America. After taking Oscar's application, a clerk posed a simple question: "Were you ever illegally in the United States?"

Oscar could have simply said no. But Oscar refused to lie. He didn't want his path to citizenship to be based on fraud. He wanted America to want him. He hoped for understanding so he looked at the man and told the truth: "Yes. My parents brought me to the United States illegally when I was twelve, and I lived there until crossing back yesterday."

"Your application will be denied," the man said mechanically.

Soon, Oscar was informed that he had received the maximum penalty: He was banned from the United States for a decade.

It felt like a slap across the face.

Oscar returned to his childhood home in Mexico and set about making the most of his time. He cleaned up the family home and got a job picking beans for about three dollars and eighty cents a day. It wasn't what he expected to be doing after graduating with a degree in mechanical engineering. In the mornings, the temperature hovered near freezing and it was hard to get his fingers around the stalks of the plants. As the sun rose, the temperature rose dramatically, sometimes passing ninety. After about six hours of picking, he was soaked in sweat, but he worked fast. He still wanted to be the best, even if that meant he was the best bean picker.

Though Oscar was now living in Mexico, his story continued to spread in the United States. One day, a US senator walked out onto the floor of Congress holding a poster-size photo of Oscar and said that Oscar was the future of America. The senator introduced legislation called the DREAM Act that would allow people like Oscar—kids who had come to the United States when they were young and who wanted to stay—a way to live here legally. Eventually, President Obama signed an order that made the DREAM Act real. Even though Oscar and the other Carl Hayden students were struggling, they actually helped change federal policy in the United States for millions of students.

But, at the time, Oscar was still banned from reentering the United States. For two years, Oscar worked in Mexico and rarely saw his family. Eventually, as a result of a letter-writing campaign by Americans across the United States, the ban was overturned and Oscar was allowed back.

Two months after his return, Oscar rode his bike by an armed-services recruiting office in a mall on East Baseline Road. He had learned to ignore the recruiting offices over the years, but now something clicked in his head.

"I can do that now," he thought. "I could enlist." And so he did.

During his training in the army, his sergeant told him to report to an administration building. When he arrived, a judge was waiting to make him a US citizen.

Oscar swelled with pride. He was finally going to belong somewhere. But it was more than that, too. He was becoming part of something bigger than himself: the army, the country, and an idea about how people should live together. He recited a pledge and the judge congratulated him: Oscar was now a US citizen.

On November 29, 2011, Oscar boarded a plane bound for Afghanistan. He looked around at his fellow soldiers and, for the first time, felt truly American.

When he came back to the United States, he decided he'd had enough fighting. He left the army and, now that he was a US citizen, decided to look for a job he would enjoy. He is currently happily employed as a software engineer in Texas.

ACKNOWLEDGMENTS & NOTES

Ten years ago, I flew to Phoenix to visit Carl Hayden Community High School and learn about its extraordinary robotics team. I was alerted to the students' accomplishments by Marcos Garcíaacosta, an Intel employee who was kind enough to write me. I am grateful he did.

I want to thank the members of the 2004 Carl Hayden underwater robotics team and their families. The Arandas, Arcegas, Santilláns, and Vazquezes welcomed me into their homes and talked to me countless times over the past fifteen years. Finally, Allan Cameron and Fredi Lajvardi have devoted their lives to helping kids achieve their potential. I remain endlessly inspired by them and their commitment to the art and profession of teaching.

—J.D.

I would like to thank everyone at FSG and Macmillan, especially my editors, Elizabeth Lee, Wesley Adams, and Hannah Miller, for entrusting me with this inspiring story and allowing me to be part of the adaptation process. I'm grateful to Joshua Davis for championing Latino stories and making sure readers everywhere heard about the incredible accomplishments of these four Mexican teenagers. Too often, these kinds of stories from marginalized communities go unacknowledged, but there are many young people like Luis, Oscar, Lorenzo, and Cristian in this country who are giving the best of themselves and constantly striving toward their dreams despite the many odds against them.

I'm grateful, as always, to my husband, Cory, and my agent, Johanna Castillo, for being in my corner and supporting me every step of the way. Lastly, I'd like to give a special shout-out to Owen Peters and Ryan Quintero. Thanks for being the first young readers to enjoy this version of the book!

—R.G.

Photographs on page iv and in the color insert following page 58 are reproduced courtesy of Faridodin Lajvardi, with the exception of middle images on the first page of the insert, courtesy Luis Aranda (left) and Oscar Vazquez (right).

Discussion questions and the boys' award-winning technical guide submitted to the MATE Robotics Competition are available at https://images.macmillan.com/folio-assets/discusion-guides/9780374388614DG.pdf

"La Vida Robot," Joshua Davis's original article about the boys and Stinky the robot, appeared in the April 1, 2005 issue of *Wired*: https://www.wired.com/2005/04/la-vida-robot/

A follow-up article, "The True Story of the Kids Who Beat MIT's Best Robots, Coming Soon to Theaters," was published by *Wired* on December 2, 2014: https://www.wired.com/2014/12/spare-parts/